LOVE
With the eyes open

The Better Expirience Is From Your On Knowledge

MB Cruz Chapa

LOVE
With the eyes open

ImagiLab.us

Love With The Eyes Open

MB Cruz Chapa Copyright ©

First edition September 2022

All rights reserved. No part of this publication, including the cover design, may be reproduced, stored, or transmitted in any form or by any means without prior permission of the author or publisher.

Photography and cover design:

>Karla Iratzel

>Nany Neferes

>Carlos M.

>Jennifer Elías

>Junior Martínez

Published by:

ImagiLab.us

www.theimagilab.com

theimagilab@gmail.com

+1 702 5595156

United States of America

DEDICATION

To God, for his light that guides me in following him.

To the true love that touches my life in such a way that teaches me not to faint, to be better, to go on, and understand that everything has a purpose.

To my loves: Armando, Nieve, Blanca, Karla, Carlos, Nany, Elías, Yayi, Tocha, Mimina, Carlo, Pepe, Neny, Armando, Dante, Ernesto, Ramón and Steve. Their patience, unconditional support, inspiration, and teachings allow me to be and improve.

INDEX

CHAPTER I

WITH EYES OPEN — 9

CHAPTER II

APPEARANCES CAN BE DECEIVING — 37

CHAPTER III

THE MADMAN MUST DIE — 69

CHAPTER IV

BUILDING A LIFE — 87

CHAPTER V

THE LAST MEXICAN MACHO — 109

CHAPTER VI

THE DOG OF THE COLONY — 135

CHAPTER VII

THE BAGS OF POOP   143

CHAPTER VIII

HEAVYWEIGHTS   161

CONCLUSION   187

GRATITUDE   193

My Story   195

BIBLIOGRAPHY / REFERENCES   205

CHAPTER I
WITH EYES OPEN

At dawn, a fox looked at her shadow and said to herself:

— Today, I will have camel lunch.

And he spent the whole morning looking for camels.

But at noon, he looked at his shadow again and said to himself:

— Well, I'll settle for a mouse.

Gibran Khalil Gibran

In every situation, our opportunity to do or not do something is mental. We tend to overreact to events in our lives because, on many occasions, our restless minds generate erroneous thoughts modeled from environments and people to whom we are exposed to fear, shame, failure, and insecurity. We become what we think; if we believe we can do something, it is because it is true; likewise, if we believe we cannot do it, it is also true. We become that which we often seek not to repeat because, unfortunately, we see it as part of us, and we stop resisting, allowing our steps to be clumsy and insecure as we advance along our path; if at one point we thought we could run through them, doubts make us lose our way, we no longer enjoy, the energy with which we started is fading, and the pace becomes slow and tired, and over time it stops flowing in the same way. We begin to settle for what we've got. We believe it is so; we begin to stop resisting, allowing the tide to take us or bring us in its own way without reaching a safe harbor, the one where we long to be for our own pleasure.

The causes of all our ills are mental; the power of our mind cannot rule us; we must make it understand that we oversee our lives and its power is ours; we must be in control and rule it.

A phrase that tells this truth is: "The mind is an excellent employee and a bad boss."

We must not allow him to dominate us; we are not his employees; we are the bosses, and we are in charge. The way to see things is with open eyes, without fear, accepting and loving who we are, being grateful for the opportunity, and making the most of this moment to go on, continue, and transcend.

The change will come from within; we will stop playing with shadows and face reality. Changing ourselves will change our environment; we will move away from what does not add, does not support, and does not promote our growth. Abandoning our limiting beliefs and internal works that sabotage us, silencing that little voice that makes us give up whenever we propose something, understanding that failures do not exist and that they are only approaches that did not work when doing something, the idea is to look for a way that works for us, thinking positively, working within ourselves, meditating, having faith, and staying in harmony with our whole being.

If I want to change my life, I must change my mind, because changing my way of thinking changes both my thinking and my life.

Being aware of the change, with the information we are accumulating, we will have the opportunity to select the right way to store it, thus preventing the fear of failure from taking hold of us again, automatically canceling "the buts, the fears, the insecurities." It is about having confidence and venturing on that path that leads us to personal success, where satisfaction will make us feel that moment full of light, peace, happiness, and love with deep gratitude, wanting everyone to feel it.

That is why each of us must work on what we build and see clearly; if we do not feel comfortable, it can invariably be changed, and we could decide for ourselves. We must be aware that every decision we make will always have consequences. Everything will be the result of something; nothing is without a reaction to what we do, think, or say, so act naturally and at the right time. Sooner or later, the consequences will come; we must be prepared for them, accepting that we were the cause and effect of this result.

Accepting is not something negative; on the contrary, it is to allow ourselves to get back on track, to take the necessary energy and propose to move forward, forgiving our mistakes and forgiving ourselves, letting the past fade away to only make it present in the moments that serve, that help us to be well and go on; we are already good and perfect, and we have everything we need to achieve it; now we go for the best, excellence, and the reward of our efforts.

To make changes, we must let go of attachments that become burdens and unnecessary weights. We do not have to accept burdens that limit us; we can always choose; therein lies the power of our choice.

To see in the right way, to be human, to love and have empathy that brings us closer to the feelings of others without falling into their vices, to learn to love in the right way, to respect individuality, to give support in the right way, to serve others with charity and humility, to raise our spirituality without falling into extremes.

I heard someone say that he had a moment of intense pain when he could perceive that his words hurt someone and sense the deep regret that his words caused. A group of young people was conversing on a street corner when a thin girl passed in front of them on the sidewalk. When she walked by, everyone heard a voice insulting her, and they all agreed to make fun of her and insult her. One of them made an offensive comment, not so strong, and that was enough to learn something that marked him definitively; at that moment, the girl turned around, and he felt her gaze piercing his heart. He felt full of anguish, fell silent, lowered his gaze, and repented. He silently asked for forgiveness and prayed that the girl would overcome the illness and problems she was going through. He learned that words carry the necessary energy to be able to destroy or build, and now he prefers to take care of them and use them in the best way.

He expressed it with deep pain on his face:

—I have stopped saying bad things about others; I used to do so, sometimes encouraged by others, joining in the general mockery where actions are not measured, and no thought is given.

—At that moment, I was able to see her emaciated face; I noticed her suffering; she was ill! I felt it; my body experienced for an instant what she was suffering. Without saying a word, she just looked at us and went on her way. My body managed to capture her energies in that look; I felt her pain and the weight she was carrying. I felt it, and it hurt me so deeply that I learned to respect it.

—Each of us carries burdens that others ignore within us, and despite that, we offend without thinking that we all suffer in some way, and everything comes back to us. I may have that condition at some point, and I would not like to feel the offenses or mockery of others, so I decided, at that time, to stop doing it!

—We met again, and we greeted each other with a gesture. I felt his forgiveness for my action; I could feel it, and I understood that this would never happen again.

We must not wait for our soul to grieve; we must act now. Doing so will bring about new changes for the better, where our eyes are opened and we can see, feel, and hear our actions clearly, observing our mistakes and correcting them before they come back at us wanting to collect the payment for our deeds. We are not prepared for what comes our way.

In this expression of something so intimate, we can have that feeling that we have ever had, and because of shame, we keep it quiet without letting it out and saying, "I was wrong!" I can change, I can be better, I will do things well and even excellent things, and I will feel its benefits as blessings that reach me and those around me.

Learning with sincere words makes us be honest with ourselves, recognize our weaknesses, turn them into strengths, and move forward without allowing the shadows to distract us with their erroneous figures that chase us. We see the others so that they do not scare us off on our own without letting us generate any change and remain in error.

To keep seeing with our limited capacity, without growing, without respect, falling into behaviors by imitation, encouraged by others who join us when they see we have no will, that they take advantage of us, and that we let them because maybe we don't want to be on the other side of the ridicule and accusations. We cannot change anyone's capacity, only our own, which comes out as learning and experiences give us the ability to overcome the way we usually see life. The limitations of everyone around us are controlling us in their own unique ways by attempting to impose on others what they have come to accept as reality. They cannot see beyond what their limiting beliefs allow them to see. In this way, they go through life judging, criticizing, giving their opinions, and mocking, because they usually do not understand what they do not know.

We all have changed ways of looking at life in this world, some more than others. However, we have all taken part in these degrading ways of acting so much that we don't see the pain of others and join voices so full of ignorance that we think we are doing good when we wave banners of justice. Systematically trying to avoid these poison-laden darts make us feel bad, embarrass us, or expose us to the public eye may hurt us in one of the many ways in which ignorance acts.

Decisions and comments should never be made when we do not think correctly; this, combined with the learning process, is full of limits that blind us to the correct way to see reality.

The difference between emotions and feelings is to learn that the former is short-lived and tends to come out automatically if we do not learn to control them. Generally, they are used to keep us safe; it is our sense of survival activated naturally.

It's where our instinctive responses of flight, confrontation, or paralysis usually take over, setting off a chain of other feelings that try to make sense of what we did. On the other hand, our thoughts are more thoughtful, thus generating attachments that tend to last longer. Even though we know that if we want to keep control of our personalities, we need to know how to use them correctly and take advantage of everything that can help us get better.

If we could see our reactions and find a way to control them, that would make us better people; we would see differently than the way we have been forced to see.

We carry the teachings of others in our eyes, the visions of those who guide us along our paths. We try to fulfill other people's dreams, which traps us with burdens that don't fit us. Although we have tried to run away, that little voice that usually sabotages everything and prevents us from accomplishing great feats has taken on so much power within us that, on most occasions, we believe in it.

It's not that it's bad; it's a voice that has kept us safe for generations; this is our survival instinct. As our evolution progresses, this little voice does so with all of us. It tries to keep our body from striving for anything that takes it out of its comfort zone.

What happens when we are children? We do not usually pay attention to it; we know the dangers naturally; however, happiness is permanent; it usually resides inside us without pauses; we are the ones who measure it, controlling it to adapt ourselves to the social reality that has been elaborated for healthy social coexistence. We set rules that make us feel equal, forgetting our uniqueness—attacking our own way of perceiving. However, the generations tend to impose their own evolving ways where the most generalized forms lie, giving rise to a way of seeing life.

Our parents did their best with the tools they had at their disposal—their repressions and conditioning, their fears, strengths, and weaknesses. They were not perfect; although they wanted to project it that way, they also had their own way of seeing life and wanted, as we all want, to do the best we can for those we love, even if we are blind or have vision problems when we see their lives. It is not for lack of love; it is because it is simply not known; you cannot talk about something that has lived with us, much less if you do not perceive it in the same way.

The shadow may be enormous in the morning, eager to devour the world with its fists, but by noon, you will be so small and insignificant that you will seek refuge.

All of us, absolutely all of us, carry within us "things" that have affected us in some way; for some of us, they have been so serious that we do not know how to overcome them. But truly, everything that has happened to us can and indeed must be overcome.

No one is exclusive to pain if you think something has happened and you can't overcome it. Look below; there are people with more difficult trials and greater needs; if you want to feel that you have it all, look above, and you will see that there will always be someone who surpasses what you are. We don't need to make comparisons; we are all different, and that diversity is how we will learn to see life.

Learning to respect others and letting others, even those we love or who love us, bring something to our lives will always be warnings that try to say something. And if they don't work for us? Just be grateful for them and look for what we need ourselves.

It is common knowledge that humans prefer to trip over the same stone as often as possible until they learn to avoid it, ignore it, skip over it, or throw it as far as possible. That is when the miracle known as personal experience happens. There we acquire the knowledge that will allow us to understand how we will pass this test, each in our own way.

How many falls does it take to learn to walk, how long does it take to learn to walk, and how long does it take to get there? Everyone in their own way, at their own pace, when we get tired of falling or learn to coordinate our bodies, or when patience and help go a long way, or the best, those words of encouragement that help us to keep going until we achieve it, even receiving applause when we do it. What prevents us from continuing like this? Celebrating the achievements and issuing words of encouragement, so everyone achieves what matters to them.

Unfortunately, we are looking for a way to taste, where we all pretend to be equal, where we are serial beings like machines that can be programmed, saying what we should and should not do—that which will lead us to success.

My parents used to say, "Each one according to his own peculiar way of looking at life:

—A well-learned trade and a well-learned university degree are equal if what you do makes you feel good and happy, that which motivates you to arrive early, do it in the best possible way, and be honest in what you do. Most importantly, that makes you feel satisfied with the remuneration.

It is not the amount of what is earned; it is how it is earned, and this will allow us to know how to take advantage of our income so that it goes according to our dreams. We cannot be enslaved to something that usually leaves balanced lives and existential voids, wanting to change when life is over. There are no second chances when life ends; the moment is here and now. Not tomorrow, not later, not that later that postpones everything.

Are you going to do something? This is your moment. Fears usually disappear when facing a certain decision, which generally takes effect by overcoming, with good habits, our reluctant nature toward those efforts that take us out of our comfort zone.

Love is an invention of evolution that makes us all very lucky. This feeling gives us the most powerful drive to do everything we set out to do, as long as we remember that the first person we need to love is ourselves. We must understand that everything around us will be well if we are well. We cannot try to help anyone if we are not well; even if our personalities differ, this has nothing to do with our being well. I know that we tend to give more than we can for those we love, but that is not true; we give what we can, what we have; if we did not do it that way, we could not do it. It's just that we sometimes tend to forget about ourselves and give everything, leaving us unprepared for their needs.

It's like I'm addicted. I'll connect with people who are like me, but I'll forget that this will have consequences that will narrow my view of things and make me less safe. There are no pretexts; I have learned that we try to evade ourselves to get over the pain, but that pain does not exist if it has already happened; we are usually the ones who bring it to the present to punish ourselves, constantly repeating this pretext that helps us to justify ourselves, justifications that make us believe that we have the consideration of others; maybe we do, but one day they get tired and listen, going on with their lives—leaving others to continue lamenting what happened to them.

Love is a pure feeling that makes us be in sync with others; we can feel their pain, and celebrate their successes; "I am well if you are well," "I suffer if you suffer." There is no blackmail or manipulation in this feeling that is real and disinterested; it seeks the welfare of those it loves.

In many books, we usually talk about love as that feeling that can do everything, that expects everything, that supports everything, and that we also tend to idealize that perfect love and perfect harmony and that they were happy forever. It is not so, since this loving tends to overcome the challenges that life presents, having the visit directed to the same place—that point that is marked and where you want to get there with support, solidarity, kindness, hope, faith, and charity—making the path of life more pleasant in this way.

It is to see how things are done for us or for others, feeling that energy that transmutes our being in every possible way, leading it to perform feats that are not thought of but only performed to feel joy and happiness.

Although we usually say that the purest love is that of a mother, we are in times when this comes from the feeling of love that one has, and that is not only awarded in this way since the pure feelings that are expressed towards others will be the indicators of the effort that is made to help those who need it, depend on us, or we can help.

On the contrary, to love is the opposite; "I love you" differs completely from "I love you"; nothing could be further from reality; although we usually perceive them as equal, it is not so; to love is "I am fine if I have you," "I want you for me," "you belong to me," and "I hope you do what makes me happy," expressions that in extreme cases often reach catastrophic situations where one is usually the one who loses the most. Jealousy and attachments become so strong that they dominate the environment. They are handled with blackmail and extremes that seek control, causing the real way of seeing life to be lost.

Many years ago, I coincided in a store with a neighbor with whom I used to exchange a few words. She arrived a little sad and started talking to the person attending the store. A woman a little older than us began to cry and to tell her story:

—"I'm sure my husband is cheating on me," she said. I know because he doesn't hit me anymore — and continued to cry.

We were both silent. I don't think we knew what to say.

She continued in tears: —"I prepare his hot water bath, give him his foot massage when he comes home from work, give him all my money.

I was utterly silent; the person in the store came out and hugged her, but she didn't make any comment either. What to say, I didn't know; it wasn't an unknown subject for me since my father used to be the typical Mexican macho, but not to those extremes, and I think my mother knew how to put a stop to it.

I was relieved to realize that we did not express anything that would make her feel like a judgment on our part; those judgments or comments that we always express, because our tongue is so quick that we do not think about what we say, and we cause more pain to those who are already affected.

On the other hand, to know how to differentiate between loving and wanting, they are not the same; they are opposites of each other. Wanting is: I want an apple, but I do not love it; I want a car, but I do not love it, and if this love is beyond what should be felt, it is also wrong to generate these attachments. To want is to give everything for possession, expecting the other party to reciprocate in the same way, and trying to pressure them to do so. There is no love; there is control, manipulation, and punishment.

Someone in a car accident where it was only a minor mishap gets out of the car, puts his hands to his head, and says: "It would have been better if it had happened to me and not to my car." It sounds crazy, doesn't it? Because if we want to learn to differentiate, let's listen with the open eyes of our being, and we will begin to change the way we are; only in this way is there understanding so that we can change.

Unlike love and want, we have fallen in love, which is where our hormones go crazy and make us feel addicted; in fact, the same chemical, physical, and biological reactions are generated as in addictions, which are usually accompanied by those rewards that make us feel good; those moments that create so much emotion, a caress, a message, a call, raise our excitement to such a degree that our hormones are triggered, which makes us see a distorted reality; this connection makes us feel that this is the person we want to be with; sparks are generated upon contact, and you can see the stars; it is not literal, but it feels this way, we want to spend our best moments by their side; we want to spend our best moments by their side; those moments that are Attraction usually plays these reactions on us. It is this way that makes us feel pleasure and displeasure, that encourages us and, on the other hand, affects us; one gives us energy, and the other takes it away. We are willing to make changes that benefit the relationship, and even more if they are reciprocated.

They act just like addicts for this reason. If a breakup is generated, both parties experience abstinence in different ways, suffering more than one; generally, this is known as lovesickness, which brings with it physical, biological, emotional, psychological, and psychiatric problems that, if they cannot be overcome alone, require medical care, therapy, and in its extremes, medication. This is when it has gotten out of a person's hands, and they need help like with any addiction or disease.

"One should always be in love. That's why we should never get married". Oscar Wilde

With this phrase, I usually understand that we must remain in love even after marriage and formalizing a relationship; this motivates us to always have reasons to do things when our inner voice wants to sabotage us.

Learning to see reality with our own eyes may be difficult at first, but it is exciting. We tend to stay with the vision that others have left marked in our lives, and it does not sound very easy to change it.

As children, we love our parents and feel that they are our heroes; in fact, we believe that adults are always right, and this is usually for our good. We are born so dependent that we do not understand any other way of seeing things. At this time, we learn to manage for the first time our strengths and weaknesses, and we adapt them to the best way they work for us. They appear or disappear as we grow; they are usually stages as we develop, or we learn to follow the path that is marked for us; we cannot choose, we do not understand, and we only do what we are taught.

Our parents hide their pains, adversities, and fears to get us ahead, where we all manage family rules that seek the best way to make it work. This situation is usually tested by events that, although normal in all human beings, usually try union and family development. Love usually establishes the tools that allow each one to contribute to their capacity to face and overcome adversities.

Going through adolescence is already a significant change for every human being who begins to judge his upbringing, the environment, the world, life itself, and the way we see things. We usually feel the power to do everything we want, to change the world. It is another important moment where we reaffirm, change, modify, or remove strengths and weaknesses. On the contrary, with adulthood, we usually have the experience, but the energy is declining, which makes us believe that we can no longer change our strengths and weaknesses. We begin to conform and believe that others are right, life is the way it is, and we can no longer act, unlike when we are children. We tend to be so vulnerable in front of others that we are left with no options, and we decide what we are allowed to do without being able to choose what we want. We can do it now; we have the age, energy, and power to do it.

Only that there are "buts" that invade us; they are generated by the walls that we have built with our imagination, those that have been raised for so long, that have become too high, that alter our vision, do not allow us to see beyond what we have been allowed, pushing away our reality, we stop being present in our own lives, living in a past that causes us pain, that we rarely tend to bring back the happy memories, and if we do, it is to avoid the sad moments that have c

We get no motives, and we let ourselves go like leaves that the wind tends to carry and bring as it pleases, falling into swamps that make us lose the movement, allowing us to spoil, accumulating stories that were not ours, that we only participated in them, and that we rarely lived in fullness, until we rot in that swamp, and we become disposable.

What doesn't work goes to waste.

What goes to waste rots.

What rots is discarded and thrown away.

We must understand that our weaknesses can become strengths as we work on them. I am not my weaknesses; I am more than that. I am the force that makes me transcend and be good, better, and achieve excellence.

My goal from now on will not be to see the good or the bad and from there decide; it is to know that I am better than that, to understand that everything good tends to become worse and that everything bad tends to become good, which leads us to be good without staying in the bad. So working on ourselves will only be for the purpose of being good, better, or excellent, with no other options that will cause us to regress.

Understanding that absolutely all of us seek to unload what we carry inside, usually those hurts that assault us, those dreams that excite us, or other things that make us happy, sad, or angry now. If we don't communicate with the right people and in the right way, the things we're going to communicate may look different than what we want to communicate. So we need to learn that there are four scenarios where we need to identify whom we need.

We must keep our communication perceptions of the social, the family, the personal, and the private in order so that we are not seen differently and, as a result, judged in ways that hurt or cause unnecessary conflicts because we are not doing it the right way.

The social, or what I want everyone to know, projects the personality and character that are presented in society with acquaintances and strangers.

The familiar, more intimate expressions of ourselves, where we tend to be more open and relaxed than we tend to be in public, where there is more intimacy.

The personal, this is where the circle becomes tighter and often differs more strongly between friends, confidants, and closer relationships that we feel confident to express our innermost personality.

The private or secret is that which is given in an intimate way, with maximum security, and which very rarely comes out because they tend to be extremely personal situations that, due to doubt, shame, or curiosity, may not have the necessary confidence to do so, or if they do, there will always be the anxiety that the secret will not be kept.

To understand this concept, you must accept confidentiality. We need to be able to act without creating postures that end up tiring us and adapting so much to our body that they prevent its natural freedom.

These ways of seeing life have been imposed on us to evolve with the least possible damage, forgetting that happiness should be part of it, creating depressed or anxious beings who do not live their present moment. By creating depressive or anxious beings who do not live their present moment, we stop being observers and realize that we are on autopilot, affecting reality. How many times do we think we forget things? How many times do we get somewhere without remembering how we did it? Bathing becomes a routine like everything else; we do not pay attention to how we wash our bodies, enjoy the water, or feel clean in this process.

Imagine that many people lose so much enjoyment from this moment that they even stop feeling the warmth of the water touching their bodies. There was a time when my body went numb. We lived in a city of constant cold, and bathing became a challenge in the wintertime, so I liked to feel the steam of the boiling water in the environment. I opened the faucet and let the water run until, at a certain moment, there was no more cold water. My body had stopped perceiving the difference of the extreme heat; on the contrary, if I could have made it hotter, I would have done it. One day I wanted to take a bath with my children, who were small, and they did not like it; they said that it was too hot, so I mixed the water with cold water, which for them was a pleasure, but for me it became a torment.

Then I realized that something was not right: the boiling water was somehow numbing my flesh so that I did not feel. I got worried and started to change this habit because, without realizing it, I had fallen into an extreme that did not benefit me.

I thought of my father; he used to bathe at any time and in any season, place, or weather at five in the morning with cold water, no hot water; it was heard the first moment he got into the water; it was already well known by my family, and although he always insisted that it was healthy, no one was encouraged to follow that habit. On the other hand, he loved boiling and spicy food; sometimes my mother said that he should eat on the stove with the pot on the stove because no matter how hot it was, he always complained that it was not hot enough. It was his way of looking at things; for him, it was not so hot for all of us; it was boiling. Ways in which we create little ways to evade our reality are something that makes our body naturally react to counteract the excesses, those that harm us, even if we are not aware of it. If someone comments, we should pay attention, and if it is not correct, just ignore it. But if he is right? Act and bring an action to the movement for change. We can all do it at any age.

There are no barriers; we can break down the ones we create with only the willingness to believe it is possible.

No one is too young or old to learn; age is a number and a state of mind. My oldest daughter often tells me, "We don't get older, just less young."

I believe you, children, grandchildren, parents, siblings, and friends, even if they are strangers, usually generate that love that makes us believe and create, feel that life can be seen differently, that we can take advantage of every moment believing that it is the best that has happened to us, and that we must see our reflection not through a shadow, but rather through a mirror that tells us how extraordinary we are, with perfect bodies that seek to transcend. May we become children! That is our innocence. We see everything in its own way; no matter if we believe we are great, of course, we are immense and must believe it. If we are adults, may we make the best decisions, do good, and generate that energy that will make the universe conspire for our benefit?

Let us learn to ask in the right way, without the shame of thinking that we do not deserve it; on the contrary, ask, and it will be given to you, touched, or opened to you; it does not say that you must ask; just ask, everything that makes us feel willing to achieve it with a genuine commitment, authentic, sincere, without buts or excuses, without postponements or limits, we are a perfect creation that has come to generate, to create, or to be happy.

Whenever I say that happiness is permanent, it is because I believe so; we do not understand how it works; it is inside us, waiting for the moment we let it free! This usually reacts with that childish amazement for everything around us, making us wonder like children, who usually enjoy everything to the fullest, do not hold back and enjoy their experiences, avoiding keeping in the present moment their damages, mistakes, or pains, but instead let them pass and move on. We are adults, and when we understand what happens to us due to parental carelessness, we usually realize something is wrong. Far from forgetting it, we take it out to flagellate ourselves again and again, repeating, in the same way, everything that happens to us, keeping this justification as a flag of defeat.

Let's learn to let our happiness prevail even in the most difficult trials. My mother used to say that they can hurt our bodies but never our minds, and these will make us better; we will overcome everything, even the damages. Your way of seeing will be the one that will help you, will save you.

And my father, if you want to feel pain, look down on those who have it, and when you feel you are superior, look up so that you feel small and end up with your ego, which does not prevent you from seeing correctly.

Now that I can no longer tell you how grateful I am to have you, I understand that in life, brother. It is impossible to do it in person when there is a gap between us. So I usually look at the sky and tell all those who have transcended a dimension beyond where I can perceive them: I fill it with blessings, I recognize everything they did for me, and I am invaded by the pain of helplessness of wanting to hug them and give them those kisses that were missing, and now I usually give my love, admiration, and respect to all those around me. It is not easy; sometimes life prevents us. Daily life tends to manage threads that sometimes make me lose my control, but I remember my power and I return to work with this being that must overcome his mediocre mentality.

Half believes it must, half believes it can, limiting my full potential where I have the faith to believe, to create, and to be able to.

With my eyes open, I can see my past without pain, overcoming this that for so many years made me feel that my value was diminished by the damage that others had caused me, mistakes that, because of their ignorance, they had made and that, in their condemnation, they will carry the penalty of their mistakes. With my eyes wide open, I seek to move away from those confused who seek to cause pain to overcome theirs, leaving their shadows to be reduced to mice, insignificant, has allowed them to lose their value. To live now is to know who I have by my side, to give them my love, and to know how to distinguish that each one must have a place without confusing the social, the personal, the family, and the private in that harmony so as not to harm myself or others that cannot understand.

Let's stop going through the world believing that others will understand what happens to us; how can anyone understand what only you have seen with your eyes, lived in your own way, felt with your limitations, seeing the paradox that everyone carries and is trying to understand? Still, it will never be in the same way as oneself. We are the best friends we can have if we learn to live with ourselves.

We can be surrounded by people and feel lonely, and we can be alone without feeling lonely; loneliness is sometimes the best companion for creativity, and that is where the best inventions and the best answers happen.

Let's stop going through life, seeing with different crystals what we must see; those who at the time helped us start our way gave us the opportunity to choose; this power is our way to use the agency that happiness is already adapted to us. Naturally, we just must use it.

We are excellent, the best work of the divine plan, of the universe, of creation, each in his own way, belief, we are incredibly perfect, we have a body covered with sensitive skin that usually perceives everything with sensors that are activated, our vision adapts to the dark or light, making us see and perceive our surroundings in that way, and the sense of smell generates another way to identify aromas and give it an image in our mind, our brain, our mind,

The magic formula is to understand how we can solve problems, that by doing so, they will cease to be problems, thus achieving the success that will give us satisfaction. Whereas luck is an ideal state that determines circumstances that may or may not benefit, understanding that one creates it, we seek it, we must be prepared as both are usually the result of our actions, so we must be prepared, and in addition to seeking luck, being prepared, we must be bold, be prepared, and generate the potential for it to exist in the right way, that is "good luck."

Our actions will create action and reaction, one of the universal laws, which, together with the universal values, will make us receive the consequence of our actions and thoughts. If I give of myself, that is what I will receive.

As I commit myself to life, it will deliver in the same way and proportion as what I do; if we want to succeed, to achieve success, not that which others put in us but that which makes us happy, to feel satisfied, it will be because we have committed ourselves to giving the best of ourselves, without faltering, without backing down, or leaving for tomorrow, with every tomorrow what we must do today. So luck exists; we create it, and if we believe we can do it or if we believe we can't, in both cases, we are right. It is true, but there are things that we still do not know that we can do and others that we believe we cannot do, but we do not know; we must engage in the effort to recognize our abilities and at any moment know that I can change my strengths and overcome my weaknesses.

The consequences of our actions demand close attention so that we realize thoughts that invite us to say, to do, to believe with faith that everything that depends on us we can do, we are perfect beings, which can always be better, we do not need anything, just define our goals well and seek achievement.

I am not a leaf that the wind blows at will; I am a seed of science, technology, and feelings, a story that has many ways to bear fruit, reaching beyond that small being and giving the opportunity to transcend to a higher being in order to do good, feel joy, and be willing to help others, without losing sight that I am the most important being, and that if I want to help, I must lead by example with my words.

To be in full awareness is to see things objectively, have the necessary faith to continue, and at the same time to recognize and make changes, not to remain static because we believe we are too old; changes can occur at any age, and sometimes we feel that these can be miracles that make us see, feel, and hear more clearly.

I am that perfectly imperfect being that constantly seeks to advance, ceasing to be those beings that go like shadows behind the future without ever getting to know it, that go repeating their past without overcoming it. Let those shadows give us a complex and let us see with our own eyes what we really are, and let us be willing to change what hurts, what we do not like, to remove what hurts, to modify, to restructure, to be good, better, and excellent, always remembering the greatness of my being, recognizing the greatness of others, respecting and wrapping my emotions in controlled acts, that my feelings are good, mainly towards me and everything that surrounds me, and to remove what we do not. Overcoming all those things that have stopped our progress, cutting them off and leaving them behind, recognizing that we are more than that, more than everything, supreme, infinite, we are perfect creation in search of knowledge and creation.

Supermen and superwomen are preparing for exaltation. Let us not allow our bodies to fall asleep under the hot water and stop perceiving; let us open our eyes, and with our eyes open, let us understand that everything has a reason for being, that we must accept it, recognize its meaning for me, and not remain still, eating the world with our fists, enjoying every moment. To embrace beyond the simple act, to make others feel that they are important and special, to transmit those clean energies until we are clean, pure, and new.

I am what I believe in myself to be; I believe in others in the same way that others have believed in me, so now I will pay more attention to my words, deeds, and ways of projecting myself. Recognizing that in perception, we can be more than that and feel more than that, beyond the poses or faces that hide those beings full of fears, anguish, failures, hopelessness, and a lack of love, we must stop believing that others are better, or more perfect, or that their lives are superior to ours. We are not equal; life is as perfect as each one manages to perceive it, being grateful for the moment and being present in it without thinking that it would be better; it is what we have now, here, at this moment, if it is not what we want if we must overcome it, then perform the actions that bring me closer to what really makes me feel successful, happy, and complete as a person, beyond the prejudices and visions of others, free and full of happiness, with a light step towards our own path, helping others.

We are all better, perfect, with tests and challenges, with fears and ideas, beliefs that limit us, that attack us; no one usually escapes that being small, playing the way of others. We just do not manage to understand that the more we grow, the more opportunities for improvement we also have; if it were not so, there would not be so many ways to help today, where we seek to find new ways that work to get us out of that mental prison that we have not been able to control and that plays us bad times. Those who, by force or by their own will, can resort, depending on the case, to strategies, recommendations, counseling, specialized centers, doctors, specialists, hospitals, medicine, therapies, coaching, and counseling, but nothing works if we are not willing to make the change that we have the willpower to make happen. The will must be real and conscious for the help to work. Otherwise, we can acquire alternatives that give us easy ways out and end up controlling more than what hurts us—drugs, addictions, bad habits, and dark desires that continue to produce a bad perception of who we are.

Life is beautiful, and escaping from all that is bad and creating our own reality can allow an opportunity among all the storms, letting us think that at any moment it must stop, that it is not forever, and that the sun must come out, without despair, without us making other decisions that will drag us more inward, not outward—letting each one do it in his own way, without ceasing to extend a hand to help those who want it.

We are the best that nature has created, perfectly imperfect beings that can achieve everything they propose in order to seek the good, the best, or the excellent; we are full of happiness and blessings; we are successes; we are achievements; we have what we owe; and we seek what belongs to us, that which will attract others who will contribute in their own way to our experience; that which we will decide, that which we will think, that we have never failed; that we have not been broken; there are only ways to learn, to be exposed, and

I am the most important person. Therefore, it only depends on me to go out and face my fears and my vices, alone or with the help I need to strive without losing faith that I can make it; even if the road fades, I will know how to find it and get to where I want to go. I will know how to live with myself, always recognizing that I am a unique and special person, full of myself, taking out what others have imposed on me and selecting within myself what I want to keep.

I am a perfect person; I lack nothing, and in my imperfection, I will no longer cause pain, neither to myself nor to others. Success will be personal and will be what makes me happy, without false expectations, in the present moment, always seeking to be better.

Light often always prevails over darkness.

After the storm, there is always calm.

Nothing lasts forever.

Therefore, it is necessary to recognize that life will have its moments and that I will be the only person who will give them meaning, trying to give them to me, helping me to have those crutches that will provide me with their help, giving me their comfort, dry my tears, change my stormy thoughts, and allow me to enjoy this moment, surrounded by those who are there, regardless of the emotional, spiritual, or mental-physical state.

I am here and now, and I have the power; it lies in me; it has prevailed; it has transcended and will continue to transcend; I generate what I attract; I am light and strength; I have dominion and control. Therefore, I am a powerful person who will overcome and achieve all that is proposed.

CHAPTER II
APPEARANCES CAN BE DECEIVING

"Strive to keep up appearances, and the world will open credits for everything else."

Winston Churchill

We tend to perceive with a distorted vision, without being able to see beyond what our eyes allow us to see; we go through life confused, giving feelings and opinions that make us feel that they are true, and we tend to get carried away by the moment or the words that others express about themselves, and we tend to believe them.

We let that gap of ignorance hit us from time to time, making us see our mistakes, which most of the time usually leaves damage in us; these can be temporary or permanent, depending on the intensity and closeness that we have formed in this type of relationship.

By way of revenge, we usually do the same with others; either consciously or unconsciously, we do what everyone else does; sometimes, I can say that there is simply nothing. However, we are the ones who are creating a story that ends poorly, leaving us deeply disappointed. In others, we believe in words and actions cease to be important. Our ear is so magical that when we hear what he wants, it alters our vision at will. As we believe in the words, as this moment passes and actions arrive, we see beings that are very different from the ones we used to see.

Sometimes we come out alive, in pieces, with little pieces of ourselves that we try to put in place to accommodate as best we can be shattered and allowing these feelings to go with us, lulling our steps, without seeing that we can leave them out. We will automatically be free, but we believe we are still prey. We go emitting our smell of fear, insecurity, and distrust, attracting others, putting us at risk of continuing to be the bait to continue being the prey; they will always be similar, with the same intentions, that seeing us vulnerable will have no mercy. We will fall into this game again and again, systematically, in a spiral that approaches and moves away, like a whirlpool of water that submerges us in depth. From time to time, we usually let ourselves out to take breaths of air to not let us die—asking, "Why me? For the simple reason that I become the magnet. I am the person who creates his reality and his environment.

By leaving those weights outside of us, we will see more clearly and learn to be alone, even when surrounded by people. We can decide whom I want to accompany us or whom I want to accompany us, without impositions or fear, simply because we choose to do so.

Without appearances, we will be more natural and see that not everything is as we have been led to believe. We will know that our decisions will have consequences and will gladly accept what we receive. If it is good, we will be satisfied and happy; if it is different, we will learn to overcome and look for the way it should be in order to receive the reward.

Sometimes we fear the "coconut," and other times we can drink its water. It depends on the way we are willing to see things, on how they really are, on how we want to see them, or on how they make us believe them. We choose; there are no pretexts, no considerations; it is as it is: you get on with life, you are the one who commands and directs the course, or you leave yourself exposed to the waves that take you and bring you at will.

I was born into a family of very opposite ideas; my parents had a powerful attraction that sparked when they were together. Both for the good things that were enough and the bad things, which were usually less, but because of the force with which they were done and the damage they caused, these were more permanent in our lives. Thus, one day, when my mother decided that there would not be enough love, the one she was tired of saying to show her, she stopped waiting for that change to happen and what she had was not enough; she said: "There are those who have so much light in their lives that they insist on hiding it; they put mud, dirt, bad actions that suffocate it, until one day that light begins to fade until it goes out and stops shining." Referring to my father, I feel that she always saw in him that good, kind, gentle, generous, cheerful man he sometimes liked to be. But he himself was determined to keep it hidden; his machismo prevented him from letting himself be seen that way by the majority; like him, a macho man, he simply could not. It was then that my mother knew that she would not spend more time helping someone who would not allow himself to be helped, let alone damage what was left of her family.

He taught us to love him, to respect him for the simple fact of being our father; he made us always see all the good, never the bad, nor the mistakes he made; no, only the good, although he always insisted on distorting with his attitudes that person that my mother saw in him and forced us to see too, without us focusing on anything else. For his part, he used to see the imposition as something that was very different from her; she did it so that we would always look for the good in others; on the contrary, it was to see the bad and never forget it. With time, the waters take their level, and in the end, we will always come out as the person we really are, or rather, the one we love the most, making known externally the reflection of our inner self.

They managed to do a lot together; they were an extraordinary couple. I think their success was based on the constant trips he made, those absences that allowed us to allow him many things by missing him and forgiving others. Seeing him come through the door, so tall, so strong, so imposing, he was our hero who did not let anyone intimidate him; that man was so tireless and full of courage that he showed himself without a cape to the world; that man was my father.

They managed to do a lot; on the other hand, my father, who is generally spiteful, never accepted the fact that she was doing well. He used to tell me that she would end up old, which was not true; finished, which was not true either; alone, even less, and without a house, money, or goods, but in these desires, he always unloaded his frustration, which I now consider impotence, and at the same time just for having let her go with his actions. On the contrary, she knew how to maintain her security and poise in any circumstance and overcome all expectations; she managed to make a living and was very happy, in her way, as she used to see life. Unlike my father, who avoided being him in front of others, he was that polite, kind, reasonable gentleman that no one imagined. What reason did my mother have to leave him?

She used to say that he was like a lamp at the door, and that when he came in, it would go out, "lamp in the street, darkness in his house." Then she would tell him: This will end up leaving you just because of your attitude; you can see life differently, let go of the past, and give yourself a chance to believe and be. Unlike my father, he never listened to her, and his words took a long time to be fulfilled.

In that opposite way of seeing life, they created very special people as children in their relationship; they gave the best of them, although this was not always good for us. We were insecure, fearful, and volatile, trying to go unnoticed, but our stature, presence, and way of being made this impossible. It appeared to be all right.

In the street where we used to live, there was a very special family that I admired: an older sister who was already working, a brother almost the same age who did not work or study, and another sister who went to school used to pass in front of the house. We coincided on the way, two very young brothers and their parents. I saw them so happy and always kind that I felt a little sad to see me with so many problems. Things from the past that hurt me a lot and things in my family that were not as I thought they should be. They had a life where it seemed like everything was perfect. One day I saw that their older sister wore gloves; she was missing fingers on one hand, and I never knew why. There was a store next to their house that sold stationery, and one day when I went to buy something for my homework, I realized that their brother was assaulting them; he was the man of the house, the males of that time. The younger sister's name was Reyna, which her brother called her at that time, and she looked like a queen, so pretty, happy, and kind. One day we heard an ambulance pass by; it parked at her house. Soon after, we could hear the screams and lamentations; she had died. Reyna decided for herself to end her life by ingesting something. I dreamed of seeing her happy, getting married, having children, finishing a career, and traveling. She deserved it. I will never understand her decision, which at the time had to be very powerful for her to make it. That affected me more; we were almost the same age, starting to go to high school, an age when we tend to suffer from everything; hormones play their role inside and outside of us. I got depressed looking for answers and found more questions. She was pretty, and I couldn't figure out what had happened.

That made me pay more attention to people; I started to see all the people around me with different eyes, and I realized that we all had some problem or situation. I had neighbors with houses, families, cars, and difficulties. Not everything was as I had perceived it before.

Most of the time, we tend to believe that we are the only ones who suffer, that we are the only ones to whom something happens, but that is not so; we do not have the exclusivity of anything. Blessed moments usually pass and never remain, as they allow us to enjoy both sides of the coin, where we are allowed to change and be different or continue in our position that "nobody loves me, everybody hates me, the whole world is against me."

I began to understand that we all do the best we can with the tools we have, that we believe our limitations allow us to need glasses, and that these have the wrong prescription, but we have no more, so we get used to perceiving in this erroneous way. My parents are the best parents in the world; they were my parents, and this fact alone has allowed me to be intense with the life I have, to believe that everything has a purpose, and to live the best I can. For this, they have my thanks.

They taught us what was in their hands and within their reach; they could not do more with their limitations; they did the best they could do, in their own way, but with their whole being. In those moments when I could see my life in that way, I could realize that there were people who lived in different conditions than mine. Where big cities are intolerant of the difficulties of others, they do not understand excuses and continue their march without being aware of the sufferings of less fortunate people.

They used to be very charitable; they were the type to take off their coats to give to others. They didn't limit themselves if this was in them. Something makes me have a chicken heart (a chicken heart gets sad about everything), so I tend to be very sensitive to this. I saw that there were people with less privileges than us, families with real problems, orphans living with their uncles, and economic needs, and for the first time, from my heart, I asked God, the one my parents have taught me is everywhere, why do you allow this to happen? I still don't understand it well, although I think everything has a reason and nothing happens without it.

Creation is so perfect that we are the ones who have not understood our power, that which makes us overcome everything; we have that power because we are daughters and sons of a God, our father in creation, powerful universal energy, and then we are gods in power, in preparation to continue, or energy seeking to transcend.

This began to keep me aware of reality, not the one I perceived before, where I was the only person who had problems; I began to realize that there are things that happen to us as children that we cannot avoid; sometimes they are oversights, opportunities that make the beasts smell them, take advantage of them, and cause us harm; sometimes we repeat them as parents; it is not because we want to; it happens in a brief moment, and we get to suffer it forever. So my philosophy is changing as time goes by; because of what I learn, because of experience, or because of my age, I see the good in everything that has happened to me; I think I can handle it; it is for me. I stop being deceived, and without justification, I am grateful for what happens to me; the beliefs that usually put limitations on me are overcome, and believing becomes my only way to continue.

Speaking of beliefs, I love to say that what I believe is because I was allowed to believe it; however, the examples and actions of all those who have been around me have swept away the teachings since what they did was more powerful than what they thought; however, there are words that surpass the actions and remain intensely engraved in our minds, constantly appearing to continue controlling who we are and avoiding whom we can become. In the end, everyone lives their learning according to their capacity and understanding.

My mother won most of the time because she spent more time with us, while my father used to have his own advantages because of the strength and authority he imposed. I can say that they did not impose anything on each other; they accepted each other that way. They didn't have that fight; they even respected the way in which each one of them tried to educate us. When was it necessary to impose something?

I can't understand how two beings so different could be so similar at the same time. Only by seeing them in their good moments was this perceived; the chemistry between them when they were happy, cooking, talking, and making plans, unfortunately, faded away when they started small fights that ended up being wars in which everyone lost, including us.

This forced us to adopt a binary system in which there were always two opposing points of view, each with their own reasons; even though their beliefs were always mutually respectful, my mother's situation forced us to adopt this system. Otherwise, I could say that everything was almost perfect if there were no differences. We are always between the rigidity of one and the flexibility of the other; it was heaven and hell, where my father was absolute, imposing, intolerant, impulsive, authoritarian, unconscious, and inclement, with his tolerant, humble, patient, thoughtful, prudent, kind, and empathetic counterpart, making us go back and forth in a game that outlines variants that are in all of us. I have seen how we went from much love to extreme intolerance by seeing the competition between us and parts of them in our faces, attitudes, and temperaments.

There used to be none. Indeed, I believe there are none, only that our vision is still affected, and we listen to those inner voices that corrupt us until we give in to them. They let us see what we really are not, and although we regret it, we always go through the same situation until there comes a time when it does not matter anymore.

We tend to see how force always prevails over reason, and this is usually encouraged by alcohol, which always ends up wreaking havoc, as well as by other addictions that are acquired to suppress our inner sorrows, addictions that we do not always notice and that damage in the same way as those that we can perceive.

I couldn't tell if my father was an alcoholic; I don't think so; what I do know is that he didn't know how to drink; he was with many people at the same time, and if he was happy, this made him happier, to the point of being euphoric, giving, giving, and saying good things to everyone. On the other hand, there was the one who lamented and was sad about something that had happened to him at some point. We all helped him—my mother, me, and especially my older brother.

My mother never drank or smoked, as far as I know. She had her moments of anger, in fact, some blows that if they touched you, they used to open your skin, slaps, but most of the time, her anger was reduced to some screams, and she used to throw whatever she had at hand, including the shoe that was the most recurrent because of the ease, and with very bad aim; I remember that once he threw some jars and he hit my sister, and after that, they were both crying, one for the hit and the other for having hit him. That's when I understood that it was like an unintentional threat, but that time my sister returned, and that's why it happened.

With my father, it was not like that. If there was something that bothered him, that made him look for a reason to explode, he would explode with whatever he had in hand, and if he had been drinking, he would hide in alcohol, making the house, not a safe place where no one escaped his fury, with my mother defending us from him and us trying to protect her from him until he would get exhausted and leave the house or go to rest, the best thing for everyone was for him to leave, usually with a brother, as it used to happen with us. If some uncle arrived looking for the pretext of the talk, they would bring out the bottles, and any reason was enough. My mother tried to keep herself isolated, oblivious to the situation, but she could never be transparent; she always sought to vent her anger, more on her, my brother, and two sisters; I don't know why she always showed so much anger. With her, it was because he was her owner and could even kill her if he wanted to; with my brother, "to make him a man;" with my sisters, I don't know; between the screams, I tried to hide under the bed with the two younger ones, telling stories or shutting them up so that he wouldn't realize where we were.

These were routines that did not change until my brother grew older, and little by little, he began to realize that this prevented him from continuing in the same way, so in his impotence, he became crueler, not out of malice but because of his demons that would not leave him in peace.

The same demons take over some of us from time to time and bring out the worst versions of us until peace returns; we repent and seek forgiveness. This came from her when my mom used to say that there is no greater pain than carrying your mistakes and being aware that you made them without regretting them. I never saw her hold a grudge, and neither did my father nor my uncles, who were able to avoid these situations many times.

It had been almost twenty years since I can say that he always provided everything for our family, which was very large, with six children who were always hungry, growing, needing school, shoes, clothes, and everything that our home required without allowing my mother to work. Although she always maintained that desire to do some business because of her restless spirit, when it came to selling what my father brought, if it was a lot, she preferred to do it so that it would not spoil or get in the way of the house.

She always took advantage of the long trips my dad used to make and undertook some things from time to time. She set up a sewing workshop; I don't know how she did it; I only remember that I accompanied her downtown, that she bought machines on credit, that we went to a department store, that they gave her directions, and that we went to another place that was relatively close to the house, where she talked to a couple. That week the sewing machines and rolls of fabric with molds arrived; my mother already had the employees, all women; some sewed, others glued buttons and shredded, and others ironed and packed. I remember we had fun with this routine after school; they played songs and music, and the house was livelier and more bustling.

We were all cramped in the house. He moved furniture, adjusted rooms, and set up his workshop; there were about eight machines of all kinds, a big table, and a piece of furniture for things; I liked that time; he came and went, he was happy, and we all helped him when he came back from school; she was pregnant with my younger brother; it was almost the school year that this adventure lasted; when suddenly one day, my dad arrived, She didn't say anything; she used to keep up appearances, so she said hello. In the evening, when everyone had left, she said she disagreed, that was all, as she didn't use to be in these crazy ideas of hers; however, when she had to leave again for a trip and not be at home much time due to her work, she left that same weekend.

We learned to sew, cut, and use the machines; our size helped us despite our age. There was an accident with my younger sister, who was not walking yet, and she put her hand in the motor of one of the machines, which at that time did not have as much security as now, and cut her finger. They went to the doctor, my mother did not stop crying, and they could not save it because it was inside the engine. However, my older brother disassembled the engine and recovered the finger, and he went running to the hospital to see if they could sew it, but they could not; it had been That same night, my dad arrived, to everyone's surprise, and seeing my mom in bed, pregnant and crying, he hugged her and told her that nothing was wrong, that it was just a finger, and that due to her age, she would not even notice. It was the calm before the storm; he already had his reason for taking that dream away from my mom.

So, it happened just before I had my younger brother; he unleashed the bomb and broke a broomstick on my mom, who was sewing at the time. She was crying, and they were echoes of sounds saying something, but my older brother stood up to him, and for the first time that I can remember, he was a being that protected his mom, with the strength that gives, and because of my mom's condition, he went on a trip again. My mother sold everything to the same man who gave her maquila, thus ending her dream. But not without leaving two machines for the use of the house, where we continued creating and learning to make everything we could think of; in fact, I was able to finish courses where I learned how to make garments better.

Calm would return the home until my mother, never still, would do something that would create discomfort in him. She loved freedom and traveling, so every weekend, she would carry everyone and take us to parks, hills, and pyramids to investigate what we could find. She liked animals, but my father did not; we used to say that not even spiders were in the house because they were afraid of them.

To my mother: she had lost her mother when she was almost two years old, so she went back and forth between her father's house, where she made a new family that she never felt attached to, and the house of her mother's sisters, on the other side of the river, where she never found her place either. He used to say that life is very cruel for a child who doesn't have a mother, that you can be left without a father, but without a mother, you have nothing; they usually protect and help you, not so the parents. I think there is some truth in those words. She loved all animals, plants, people, and music; she was cheerful, hardworking, kind, and with character, but with a lot of nobility, she preferred to suffer herself than someone around her. She liked to learn everything she could; she was good at writing, editing, history, and poetry; she enjoyed reading, and she said that a good book could make you change your place with its story. She only finished elementary school, but she used to say that elementary school in those days was worth more than a career in today's times, and I think I agree. She was born on the border of Mexico and the United States, so she learned many ways of doing things and saw life in the diversity of the two countries.

She was honest and hard-working, with business acumen. She had many abilities: she could save any animal or plant; she could sense something, just like me, where we can know that something is not right or something is going to happen not very well; she liked to listen to people and to help by always giving. She was short in stature and very pretty, although when your friends talk about your mom, it is not very nice for me when they express their admiration for her: she is my mother. She believed in God and liked to do it in her own way, without pressure; although she converted to many religions, she did not remain in them. She liked to forget the damage she had suffered. She liked to eat and prepare all kinds of food; she liked to set the whole table as well as the mealtimes. She loved to play; there was always a game at home in which she participated like a child; her laughter was contagious, and her jokes made you laugh; for me, it was the daily way of being at the table. She used to not take life seriously.

She was clean in every way, thrifty, used to be enterprising, and always had money. With or without my father, she managed to do a lot. More than some of my siblings won't be able to, and I had to fall back on what they both left. He neglected his body when he no longer found meaning in life;

he let himself go without anger or annoyance; he believed it was his time and abandoned us; he left us orphans of his beautiful presence, preventing my children or their children from meeting him in person. He liked to walk and do all kinds of exercises that had to do with stretching, including squats and crunches. His punishments were squatting, a series of squats, or crunches.

So, she learned to be herself, kept her madness, and didn't wear masks that changed her natural beauty. This made many people love her and some people jealous, which hurt for a little while, but she got over it quickly.

To my father: when he was a child, his life on the ranch was marred by the beatings of his father and uncles, who were not afraid of his heart and, from a very young age, forced him to leave his mother's lap so that he could become a man. Woe to him if he did not obey!

On one occasion, he used to say that he heard a cry calling him; it was his father; everyone was asleep in the house. Without further ado, he said, "I want a light," but there was no coal burning at that hour. So, not the first time this had happened, he had to go to his uncle's house, across the hill in the lands near his own. To imagine that is scary; now, at his age, as a child, you usually see everything bigger and scarier. Well, he had to go and cross a river that bordered the house, get wet with the cold that usually exists in that place, cross the hill, get to the house at that hour, and say, "Uncle, it's me, Armando" so that he wouldn't shoot a bullet and attack him thinking he was a thief. A light would come on, and immediately Uncle Francisco would show up without asking what he wanted. At that hour, he would hand him a cigarette and send him on his way with the usual "lash," that horse's "whip" that has many extensions, the one that, if it touches you, takes more than one blow to reach its destination.

He was very clean, hard-working, honest, loyal, and kind, with a complex character but a good person; he used to take life very seriously. He did many things around the house, from minor repairs to building a wall, while also participating in the cleaning, food preparation, and raising of the children. He loved cars, guns, learning what he liked, and reading, which allowed us to have a house full of all the books we could enjoy since we were very young. He used to tell countless stories that allowed the mind to see them as real in the imagination, and he played the harmonica very well. He didn't like animals, but he allowed us to have them.

She didn't have a lot of patience, but it took her to help my mom with the pile of kids. When she brought another child home, she put someone there to help her permanently on many occasions. She liked games of chance and board games. We learned to play quarters to throw coins, and the ones within a hand's length win; chess, dominoes, Chinese checkers, English checkers, Chinese sticks; any kind of game in the Spanish deck; and the classic cards. He enjoyed walking long distances and riding bicycles, preferring them to cars.

Eating was his passion, not as gluttony; he was not obese, somewhat robust but not obese; people who saw him used to ask: What is he eating, is it very tasty, has he not eaten for days, or they definitely thought he could be cheap; there were those who, when they saw him eating in a restaurant, asked for the same as him. He enjoyed life in his own way. He was a joker, a lot. Only that they broke him, also my mother, but he did not know how to resist, and those damages always remained as shadows of confusion that altered the way he saw life in a way that made him see enemies in everyone, even in his children, the different women who passed through his life, including my mother, Demons of jealousy, mistrust, and disunity that separated him from everyone and in the end, not even before he died, allowed him to leave a healthy approach, until he could no longer and was forced to not want to die alone, his greatest fear was presented in front of him, and he no longer had the physical strength to resist. But he always wore a mask that made him look sane; he used masks depending on the situation; no one ever saw anything wrong with him; only those of us who knew how he could change at certain moments knew this.

Imagine how two people like that came to cross their lives; it is not easy to understand; it is the attraction that takes over two people and makes their madness a blind love; it is that addiction that makes you crazy, and their madness spills honey in words.

Seeing them together was to feel that they were the perfect couple; they made a good combination of genes in us; although both already had previous relationships with failures, they decided to try, and I was pleased with that decision, which is why I can tell my stories that can help others to be better and see that life is the opportunity in which there was always a respect for what my parents believed; it was opposite, it was different, very personal in their perception, they never tried to impose anything on each other, now I understand that it spoke of maturity; however, when it was time to make us believe, it happened in a very rare way; between them I never saw a bother for their type of beliefs; my father, on the conservative side, always accepted his beliefs, which passed through generations in his family and that it was the only way to get closer to God.

Born in Mexico, near the capital, we can recognize the custom that was had, since in the patron saint festivities usually comes out all the fervor of the believers accompanied by established rituals, a market of holy cards, bouquets, and objects that speak of the situation, and the richest thing for me in those times was the food. I don't remember many things, but they were always sermons that I rarely understood, maybe because of my young age or because I was never really attracted to it as the years went by. This was not very frequent; it was only when my dad could spend time at home with us due to his work, and not always either because they are events that take place every year. If there were not these events and he was at home, I used to accompany him to his "mandate." We would leave the night before and walk until dawn, arriving at our place, and when he finished his business, we would go to breakfast. So when he said he would do this, we would gladly accompany him, but if it were something regular, I would show my boredom immediately. With his thunderous voice, he would say, "God will punish you, sweetheart, if you don't pay attention to the sermon." That is good; in bad times, it was a blow that made it clear that you had to be attentive, and there was no breakfast, so I was not particularly eager to go to the lecture.

For me, he was a man of great faith; he used to pray at dawn; he had that habit both in the morning and at night, before going to bed; he also had his routine, prayers that always said the same thing, and that by dint of repetition I still remember quite well; there was nothing else, it was just that. I didn't see any sense in it for me, but he was my father, our father, and he had to be respected. It was his way; that's how he was; that's how he had learned it. However, his upbringing won him over, along with his demons that used to arise many times, affecting the family environment; for her part, when my mother realized it, she tried to make him understand that this way of being was not right, Sometimes it worked, but they were the least; his being would change quickly, and fury would take over him, hurting everyone who was within his reach, although on certain occasions he could pick it up. If he reached you, you would suffer the consequences.

My mother used to refer to this with a phrase: "To God, praying and with the gavel giving." When she calmed her fury and peace returned, she let him know that God did not like it that way, that she did not like it that way, and that he would see how his children were going to remember him. Little did she care when her reason would not accept words. She often managed to control him; in others, she became prey to the behaviors she always lost; my father's strength and power always used to impose themselves both in actions and words.

For her part, my mother was also a woman of faith who was born and raised on the border, so in her coming and going between the two countries, she learned many things that benefited us. The two cultures in those places did not have the extremes of Mexican sexism, so she did not know much of this. For her, chauvinism was the one that showed her the golden cinema of the Mexican films and romanticism was the one that always had the American films where, although they talked about villains, heroes, and problems, there was always a couple that overcame everything. Personally, I think she enjoyed more the Mexican cinema because of the charros. She was very cheerful and loved music and dancing, so in her beliefs she had the freedom to decide to believe in God alone, without religion, which made her a prisoner of a single guideline, unlike my father, who only prayed in the morning and at night. She prayed constantly, for everything, and they were like talks; she would tell us that you can ask and thank God for whatever you want; God listens, and if they are sincere, they will be answered. So it didn't matter if you were kneeling, standing, sitting, or lying down; you could take a moment and thank, ask, or tell God whatever you wanted. However, she was so noble that over the years, she converted to any religion that contacted her; I do not know if she could not say no or because she believed that some might have the truth or out of simple curiosity. Although she did not remain in any of them for a long time, she made a lot of friends who used to visit her to talk to her.

The first time I remember it, I didn't know what a belief or religion was; it caused me to learn it. One day he had a visit from a lady who lived on the corner of another street; her house was very different; she used to have lots of things; my father used to refer to them as "vineyards," a term that for him was derogatory because in her house they had mountains of glass bottles, cardboard, newspapers, cans, old furniture, and lots of clothes that were everywhere. With them was a pack of dogs that we thought before we met them was for protection, but later we learned that they did not tolerate seeing animals in the streets suffering. For my mother, we were all the same, so she was pleased with the visit and invited her to come in; she stood firm at the entrance of the house; I don't know if it was out of embarrassment, discomfort, or distrust, but she did not enter the house.

The following was presented: "Mrs. Malena is at your service, your neighbor.

a lady who wore about five skirts at the same time with a bandana holding her hair shorter in height than my mother, and my mother was also petite in height.

In the conversation, Mrs. Malena was direct. She told him about a lovely place on Sundays where he could go with us; she told him where the place was and that it would help us a lot to live with other children, that if she wanted, she could also accompany us, or she and her family could take us, leaving him time to do his things.

They said goodbye, and the following Sunday, my mother got us up, bathed us, changed us as best she could, and combed our hair as if we were going to a party. We did not know what was going on, but we knew we were going somewhere, so we were excited about the idea, and so it was, there was a knock on the door. There was Mrs. Malena with her family, all well dressed, wearing slippers for women and a tie for men, all well-dressed except her; she looked clean; I can say that she was not slovenly; on the contrary, it was simply the way she dressed, very out of the ordinary. We went to the "chapel," it was for three hours, in which they were looking after us; in fact, at the end of the first hour, one of them used to be our teacher along with other people, something like a nursery where there were games, activities, crafts, songs, and more fun. We loved it; it became a Sunday routine until my older brother could be a member. It was a religion; he had talks in which he could be baptized when he was eight years old, but his parents had to authorize it.

My father knew that this lady took us to a place on Sundays because, when he was at home, we told him that we would go with them to the chapel; he never objected until it was time for the baptism. My mother told my father what was happening, and a world war broke out in our house. We did not understand because of our young ages, but we understood that we could no longer go to that place. My father objected; many relatives we did not even know paraded through the house, and my grandfather, my father's father, only remembered having seen him a couple of times. There he was talking about hell and heaven, good and bad, with our mother, uncles, aunts, and friends who did the same until there was someone who would help us get out of mortal sin; we were required to go regularly to the church of my father and his family, we were imposed under threat not to talk anymore with that family, Mrs. Malena gave us a Bible, a book with a blue cover with a trumpet player on the cover, and a book of hymns that went back and forth for years in our house. That subject was never touched again. Our vision had been managed by others, who, with their impositions, altered our way of seeing life.

I did not know well about my brothers or sisters, but I lost a place where I felt happy; we helped in its construction on the days we did not have school; my older brother climbed partitions for others to build walls; and we women took water and food to the workers, always with them taking care of us so that nothing happened to us. What was wrong with this? On the contrary, our learning was reinforced.

As the years went by, we stopped going to my father's church; we only did it if necessary. Otherwise, my mother did not force us. Still, both my father and his family, from time to time, came to visit as if they wanted to know if we did not obey the rule that was imposed on us and went running with the gossip to my father; I think my mother felt vulnerable, without family in that big city and full of children. Her only consolation was that no one had contact with her of those people, because with others she always managed to have followers, more than friends, who liked to talk with her, a kind of therapy, always ready to help, to listen, to do good, between her work and those moments she was spending time with them.

There was a lady who was mute; she went many times to "talk" with her; they were guttural sounds, signs that my mother had to guess until they learned to communicate; at least once a week, she went to see her; among other people who began to tell her that she had powers, they brought her little animals that were hurt—birds' nests, rabbits, chickens, dogs—that somehow she took care of, as well as the plants—everything she planted, grew, and bore fruit.

At a time when I felt that my life was losing its meaning, I questioned everything that happened to me; I tended to rebel; my father moved us to a bigger house that his brothers and their families flanked, one of my father's brothers over there, another one over here, and another one over there; it was something like spies that gave him an account of what they could realize. My father was always a good provider, and I can say that the house, food, clothing, and comforts we could have, in his own way, he gave the best he could, but there was not such a good environment with him.

My mother taught us that, no matter how good or bad our father was, we should still love and respect him, which seriously altered our perception of him, and even after many years, he continued to affect our family environment to such an extent that we did not know how to live together as siblings.

One day there was a knock at the door, and it was a family friend who came to visit with two people who called themselves missionaries; my mother attended to them very well; however, at a certain point, they began to preach, to which I did not give them credit; on the contrary, my questions were more and were frustrated by my mother and my older brother, Armando, who questioned my behavior. I went to my bedroom and did what my mother had always taught me: to talk with God, with that supreme being, with that universal energy, with the universe, to listen to my sorrows; I asked him: Where are you when I or others suffer? Why don't you manifest your power and destroy the wicked? I fell asleep with these thoughts. I knew that I was very blessed and that, both in the neighborhood and at school, I could perceive that I had much more than most, yet something kept me from being fully happy.

I had to leave school because of a very unpleasant event with my father that marked not only my body but also my personality and affected his relationship with my mother and the whole family. They had an attraction that produced sparks when they were together; we were so happy in their good times; everything revolved in complete harmony; they changed drastically to the volatile character and mood of my father; I have well recorded in my mind events that made me loathe Christmas, which I will explain below.

Now we will concentrate on the fact that now, with these missionaries who came to our house and now that we were older and with more knowledge, we were able to confront my father so that he would let us convert to this new religion in which we felt good and that, by a coincidence of the books that Mrs Malena once gave us, it turned out to be the same religion. I could have answers to all my questions, and at least I had a different path than the one imposed on me. To be converted, she demanded that we go to her church before going to ours, and so we did; we would go just after getting up in our pajamas with shawls, sometimes even with quilts and pillows; we would arrive, we would settle in the pews, and go to sleep again until the priest would come and wake us up; he would say that the sermon was over; we would arrive home; my mother had already had breakfast; we would bathe; get ready; and go to the chapel. I felt

There was an occasion when we coincided with my dad, and we all went together, well groomed, bathed, and awake, to church with him. At the end of the sermon, the priest approached him happily, greeted him, and congratulated him for the "so" faithful children he had; he was overjoyed. He was so happy that he gave us an incredible day.

I still had school pending; I thought that with all I knew, it was enough; however, thanks to my mother, she forced me in a good way to finish high school, and as I was ashamed to go back to the same school, she sent me to her father. My grandfather Mingo (Domingo Chapa), whom we only met twice when my father took us to visit him, lived on the border a few steps from a town on the other side, and I had the opportunity to visit him when I was there, it was February, the course was almost over, but I did not care, if there is something I have is that I really enjoy school, study, and learn, so it was not difficult for me to finish and even though I did not attend for months,

As my way of seeing things changed, it allowed me to be better. My grandfather did not let me attend my new religion because it was three hours away from where we lived, so it also did me good; there in that house, nobody talked about God, but they led good lives. In fact, when they asked me how they live there in the capital, I said, "In the capital." How does your father treat them? Silence took hold of me, and that silence saved me from giving any answer. There was an uncle who was two meters tall, and as much as he loved me, I could not stand so much attention, not because I was ungrateful but because I did not know how to accept that attention myself.

The course ended, and I went back home; I never had the opportunity to thank them for all the good they did me, although sometimes they say that it is never too late. Sometimes we wait too long, and some can no longer receive our gratitude; they have already left this life. So that waiting when it is too much leaves us with words unspoken, drowning in our mouths, making silences harder because they do not let us give that hug, gift, or words to those who somehow have done us good, have helped us, or have supported us. Known or unknown are beings who, like us, have seen life with a different vision than what it is, living in the past with other people's stories that tell us what we should do and how eyes open in the way of others, with their visions presenting an altered reality and avoiding seeing our present.

To open our eyes and keep them that way is to change the crystals that have been adapting to us; it is to allow us to see that our parents or caregivers were people who, like us, also had their stories; if we remove a little, we will see sadder events than those that hurt us. They, like most of us, tried to escape, to look for ways out that would give them a little peace and happiness, and what they thought was the closest thing to that, that is what they stayed with, staying there without expecting more, without expecting more, without expecting more, without losing illusions, dreams, and goals that we all have at some point in our lives.

I cannot say that my life has been difficult because I learned to turn the page and continue. If I want to feel the pain, I call on my past, and with it, I usually find reasons that previously had no explanation, and I can cry without rest, focused on what hurt me. That is no longer for me; I have learned to realize that looking around me, there are people who have lived through similar situations, similar or worse, and some have overcome them; the worst thing that can happen is that they do not overcome it, and the same story is being repeated daily, constantly living, being trapped in a circle without end that allows us to go as entities in life, without understanding that this can change and that in us is the power.

Mrs. Malena, a woman that few people would have accepted in her life, was able to share something very special with us that personally did me a lot of good. I do not think that was only for my family and me; I think that what seemed good to her, she tried to share it with everyone she could.

A story that I lived closely about her There is a custom that is practiced by most Latin people that when a woman is going to be fifteen years old, they look for godparents, people who give money or a very special gift to celebrate that memorable date. So a neighbor invited her to be her godmother; the girl did not want a party, said she did not want anything, and in the end, she said she wanted a piano, a gift that is not common and much less cheap.

He gave them what they wanted, and she was able to prove that appearances can be deceiving. They told Mrs. Malena about it, and she and her mother and daughter went to see pianos in the street in the center of the city. There the girl chose one, the one she liked the most; Mrs. Malena took her hand under her countless skirts and took out a bundle of money from among them, which was tied like a bag where she carried the money to pay, Without asking for a discount, she made the payment in cash, agreed on a delivery date, handed the bill to them, and left the place. Everyone, including even the seller, was left with their mouths open; they never expected that such a poorly dressed, insignificant woman could buy anything, much less a piano. Everyone was happy to get something from her; when she came to my mother to tell her about the experience, she liked to say that there are people who see material things as something that will make them feel good or happy at that moment, without knowing the true value of what it is really to be well or happy, and that these usually act as placebos for the majority who try to feel things as means to achieve it, those moments that are the closest thing to feeling good or being happy.

Things become more precious than people to them; that is their reality; that is their way of perceiving life; by choosing her, they did so for two reasons: one, to embarrass her; they knew perfectly well that someone living in the conditions she lived and dressed in would most likely not have the resources, so they could make fun of her or try to embarrass her, like saying, "We want you to be the godmother, but you can't. The other one was that in case they wanted to make fun of her or try to embarrass her, like saying, "We want you to be the godmother, but you can't. The other one was that in case they wanted her to be the godmother, they would want her to be the godmother, but she could not. The other was that in case she wanted to, she would probably be indebted for a long time with something that they were not even going to use since nobody studied piano, and so it was; she only became an object of adornment for them, something that they would never have imagined having, and they wanted to generate that commitment; they tried to put her in debt in order to make themselves look good.

Nothing was further from the truth; she could pay for the gift without resorting to loans, and she could do it simply because she wanted to do it. It was herself at all times, with her countless skirts on and her bandana on her head, that showed that being different, living differently, does not make you less than anyone else; on the contrary, the work that is done, the results, and the fact that you feel good do not have to offend or embarrass anyone. To see it that way speaks more of those who point than those who perform it.

If looking down makes me thankful for everything I have, looking up makes me see how small my shadow is next to others.

Feeling at the top should make me feel that I have fewer problems than others and that I have been able to overcome my fears and my limiting beliefs and leave them powerless in my life. Feeling at the bottom is meant to generate in me the desire to continue and the idea that each step I take is one less toward my destination and that no matter how big the mountain is, at some point, I will be able to reach the top and rest.

At dawn, I will see that I can eat a camel; at noon, with a mouse, I will be satisfied, and maybe I will arrive at dinner without having eaten a bite, trying to find my camel or my mouse, not seeing everything that goes beyond my own shadow. Opening our eyes allows us to see our environment more clearly, without allowing our vision to continue seeing what others see or make us see what others want us to see.

The decision is in each one; to see a problem or an opportunity, to see something bad or something that can serve us, to place ourselves in the positive or the negative, is our decision; until we decide, we are already deciding. Open your eyes, see, and enjoy everything that God, life, the universe, and creation have for you at this moment; the past is over, the future never comes, and what you have left is to live in the present and be present at this moment; your escapes from it are only to meditate, thank, and find meaning in your existence.

In a certain way, what we believe in appearance will be an ephemeral moment that ends without creating a permanent feeling inside us.

Sometimes we tend to leave clothes or shoes for that special occasion, but as soon as they arrive, they don't fit, or they got spoiled by the confinement. When I was very young and recently married, I used to keep things for when I had my own house, everything I thought could be useful, until one day someone came and told me to accompany her to a funeral, so I did, we went, and in the place, which was the house of the woman who had died, it was very simple, it was under construction, you could see things stored in boxes, I did not pay much attention to them, we gave our condolences, waited a moment, and left the place, soon after I found out that the widower remarried just a month after his loss, which seemed normal to me since it is more difficult for a man to remain alone, I thought, with my ignorance of what I understood at the time, you can A short time later, the same person who asked me to accompany him to the funeral visited me, and between talks, he told me that he had finished building the house and that all the boxes were things for the house itself: furniture, arrangements, kitchen utensils, bedding, and other things. As she left, I was left wondering, "What am I keeping?

There were times when I lost things, others when I believed that those same things were more important to me; in the end, everything passes and ceases to have its value, even coins before a devaluation, not life, food, or basic necessities before a calamity. We could not eat a dress, take a pair of shoes, or cover ourselves with a chain, much less embrace a cell phone. We lose sight of the value of things. In the grave, we will not be able to enjoy what we have done, but others will do it without so much effort. Every moment must be lived with those people, even if we are ourselves full of love, charity, generosity, care, and empathy; in the end, it is there where there will be a real reward.

We all used to go to church as a family; my children used to go with me. It was three hours in which all of us joined our energies for the same purposes, concentrated in the same place. Every Sunday it was normal, but sometimes the tiredness of the week allowed some or all of us to skip that habit and stay at home resting and living together. On one occasion I went on a trip, and I could not be calm; my famous anxieties made me restless. That Sunday afternoon I received a call from them, and the house had been robbed. The first thing I asked them was, "Are you all right?" To which they answered in the affirmative. When I returned, I could see the empty house: shoes, TVs, microwaves, everything they could carry, valuables, and money that were in a safe that we had never put in since the house was rented. I felt sadness, but no one had stayed home that day. To imagine that something happened to them, to imagine it, would alter my sanity.

My eldest daughter, who was married, already had my grandson. She went to church with her brothers and sisters; when they returned, they saw the dramatic picture, they called the police, they filed a report, and it was never resolved. There were many things that I did not need; I had my family, with which I felt, and I feel blessed. Things come back, but the ones that matter, no. I could not sleep at night. At night I could not sleep; I would put an armchair in front of the main entrance, even my grandson's walker, to hear any noise that would alert me. We moved to an apartment for more security. The fact here is that I think I know who was the person who did this; I hope I am wrong; the signs were clear, and the mistakes we make lead us to the mouth of the wolf, which in sheep's clothing approaches us lending help, making us believe and trust without imagining how malicious they can be or the damage they can cause, exposing us without thinking about it and without need.

When this happened, I started thinking about the people who leave everything for the American dream—the people who, in a natural catastrophe, lose everything, or in an accident that not only leaves material and personal damage but can also leave marks that you have to live with forever. That is why I look down and realize how blessed I am and look up and give thanks for how blessed I am; in the losses, some lose more than I have lost, and I am thankful that what happens has a reason, and if it happens to me, there is something to be learned from it that I must learn for my personal benefit. There will always be worse things than what happens to us. To change it, we must see it in a way that benefits us the most. Did we get robbed? Yes! What's next? Did we lose something? What's next? With or without us, time takes its course; whether you understand it or not, whether you accept it or not, that is unstoppable. You just must accept and follow, see what is in that teaching for you, and keep it to try to prevent it from happening again. I remember that on two occasions, they wanted to steal our car, but they could not. Those were warnings that I did not see; they were moments that told me that this was not our place; I did not listen to them; I did not move house because sometimes changes are tiring and we had just arrived there; we had already arranged everything. For not listening, there was a bigger noise that made me pay attention and that took away my tranquility for many days.

My father used to say that between ten o'clock at night and five o'clock in the morning, to go out on the street was to put yourself at risk, ready for something bad to happen to you; the darkness of the night usually allows some people to take advantage of this opportunity. But what happened to us was during the day, so now I add: there are certain times of the day or night when we can expose ourselves; we must see the warnings, keep care, and understand that the most precious treasures are people, and that there is no greater good that can bring back that being we love or that others love. Everything has a reason for being, so let's just accept what comes to us with gratitude.

"In the end, everything happens for a reason, and at the same time, if it doesn't happen, it is also for a reason, so apart from opening our eyes wide, we must try to perceive the intentions, the energies, and hold on to the good thoughts to move forward in any situation."

CHAPTER III
THE MADMAN MUST DIE

How did I become crazy?

So it happened: I woke up from a deep sleep and discovered that all my masks had been stolen.

— Yes, all the masks I had made for myself; I ran maskless through the crowded streets, shouting: Thieves, thieves, thieves, damned thieves!

Men and women laughed at me, and when they saw me, several people, filled with fright, ran to take refuge in their homes. And when I arrived at the market square, a young man, standing on the roof of his house, pointing at me, shouted:

—Look, he's a madman!

I raised my head to see who was shouting, and for the first time, the sun-kissed my naked face, and my soul was inflamed with love for the sun, and I wanted no more masks! And as if in a trance, I cried out: -Blessed are the thieves who have stolen my masks! And that's how I became a madman.

And in my madness, I have found freedom and security; the freedom of loneliness and the security of not being understood, for those who do not understand enslave a part of our being. (fragment)

Gibran Khalil Gibran

We never think that we are all crazy until the differences give us away, each in his own way and in his own reality. It is not enough to open our eyes and see with our eyes wide open; it is also to accept the reality that is presented to us without thinking that because we are different we are bad or that we should be ashamed of it. On the contrary, we should be happy for the uniqueness of our being, and pretending to be equal only leads to chains of bitterness that make us suffer. We are born unique and special, no matter what physical characteristics we possess. Each one is beautiful in his or her own way, and there will be someone special who can see it.

I can say that we were born to good parents. Both with their very particular ways of seeing life that made a mixture of ambivalences within us, I do not think we were bad; on the contrary, I feel that we have been too good, but with wrong decisions that, in their mistake, have paid high prices in errors.

If I lost any mask I had made for each occasion, I felt naked in front of others, and shame overwhelmed me; I had no security; although I had a strong character that evolved to become irascible, I felt like my Dulce Amarilla, a very small Chihuahua dog that we rescued, in fact, there were two of them, her and her little sister Brownie, who unfortunately could not survive due to her age and the dire conditions they were in

We followed the sound until we could see where it came from; they were two little honey-colored dogs, so small that they both fit together in one hand, not very graceful; one was prettier than the other, and both squinted with their eyes farther apart than normal. A person approached us and told us that they were animals that were not useful because they are forced to be miniature. Surprised, and in my eagerness to know more as is my habit, I asked: What happened to them? They told us that their mother did not survive the birth and that another puppy, a male, died with her, that the owners used to leave them without food so that when they were malnourished, the babies came out smaller and were sold at a better price, that the dogs, in their desperation of hunger, usually eat their own poop, causing diseases and parasites both in them and in their unborn babies, and that this can physically affect the puppies

Only that they caught us and we could not escape; we wanted to take Brownie, who appeared to be healthier; however, Dulce did not stop crying, and her barking broke our hearts, and we went for more money, returning for the two; we left to guarantee what we were carrying so they would not go to sleep in case something came across and closed the store; we returned as fast as we could, and we took them home. They were so small that at the beginning everything was tender. We took them to the veterinarian, and he told us that they probably would not spend the night and that at the most it could be a week, that their conditions were critical. He gave them medicines for infections, for parasites, for anemia, and a thousand other things, along with special enriched food. We had to make porridge and milk to feed them. Although they were babies who still needed their mother, they already knew how to eat by themselves. He taught me to inject them behind their legs to not lose the hours of their medicine. When night came, we put them in their little bed, and we were with them for a while. They did not want to eat, and to everyone's surprise, when it was time to do their needs, they fought to eat their poop and defended it as if it were their only food. They barked and got angry with each other. So I decided to put them in a closed suitcase where they had no space, neither to fight nor to eat their poop. A week later, unfortunately, Brownie died; she was the strongest and looked healthier. My Dulce was left, who together with another Chihuahua puppy we already had at home, called Muffin, brightened up many days of our lives.

The story of Muffin: It was a gift that we wanted to give to my youngest daughter, who was suffering not very good events due to the separation we had with her father, so my idea was to go look for a puppy for her. We arrived at a place that she investigated, we knocked, and at the time of entering, a litter of chihuahuas arrived. How to choose one if they were all beautiful? My daughter put them all on her lap, and one by one, they got off her lap, and only one was left; he was determined to go with us, and so it was; we did not choose him, she chose him. Muffin was bigger in age and size than Dulce, but they were both very small. Dulce overcame all her problems; she adapted to the family, and although she never lost her way of taking care of the food, she was brave if we served her food and someone wanted to get close to her. It makes you laugh, but it is sad to know that you have suffered so much hunger that you never stop thinking that at some point there will be no more.

Both were such good pets; they went everywhere with us, in our handbags; they didn't bother us; they were very well behaved; and even going to the movies with them was not a problem. However, we had to adopt two others to balance the number of members of our family, four in total, who also arrived in very special situations.

These events led us to rescue as many animals as possible, so in the end, I set a rule that we broke a few times: only the animals that arrived at the garage could be rescued following this protocol and taken to the vet. We even had agreements and discounts for our work, which involved the people we worked with and customers searching for homes that would allow them to be received and loved as they deserved.

We would not have time to capture every story that we lived more than sixteen years have blessed us with this beautiful experience, which only two or three have not managed to overcome this moment, mostly dogs, cats, rabbits, and birds, have allowed us to teach by example the respect for life, events have been made in which help is shared with others and awareness of how vulnerable we are all beings at some point. There is a phrase that is placed where we work that says: "If you need it? Take it, if you don't need it: Donate it," next to a coat rack that invites either action. Between rescuing dogs and some help, we give to the community, I must say that I or my family and more people support these efforts that give a little comfort to someone in need. Several people have become so accustomed to asking that it is hard for us to know who is really in need; I know that shame can make us not ask for help; what shame is? A simple fact that confronts us is that many times we are not immune to ridicule or criticism from others, and we stop wearing masks that show our true personality that is far from being bad; on the contrary, we are beings who are experiencing in this world, in this life, that sometimes we fail by our nature but that we can recover quickly and overcome if we so choose.

We may have suffered as much pain as those beings that cannot speak and say what has happened to them, but we must forgive any aggression and continue to believe in people.

There is a joke that I want to use to express those talks about the beautiful hearts that animals, in this case, pets, usually have. They say that if you put your husband, partner, lover, or friend in the trunk of a car along with your dog and leave them there for a couple of hours, who do you think will be happier to see you when you open the trunk and let them out? That's how beautiful their hearts are.

It is like that of children; they forgive as many times as their innocence allows them, and they comfort you when they feel your pain. My Dulce, when she saw me crying, would come close to me, turning around, wanting to comfort me; or if my children were playing games and pretending to hit me, she would come out with her small size in my defense; she felt like a lion when it came to protecting me.

We are growing up, even those of us who keep that childlike heart. However, other people want to attack us with comments that say that. You look like a child. As an offense, for me, it is a compliment. Imagine being like them again. I would love it if you saw life through childish eyes that did not understand evil, work, or money. However, at that age, we can make them suffer, breaking their little bodies, but we can never break their childish spirit.

As we grow up with pain, we find it hard to believe again, so we pretend that everything is fine. We wear masks that have become part of us, masks so well molded that even when we take them off, it seems that they are still there. Our soul is all anemic; not only our body needs care, but also our mind, our actions, and our words; we are under universal laws and values that tell us what is good and what is not; no matter how much we disguise it with beautiful, attractive, and corrupting exteriors, in the end, pain and discomfort will betray our minds and drown us in misery.

In our desperation, we eat poop; we have no other alternatives; that is what we are driven to; they want to destroy our personality and character in order to please others; it is under their terms and conditions that we can be accepted, no matter if our souls are anemic, if our hearts have infections, or if our minds inhabit parasites, social norms, and fashion; the currents of the moment demand it, and no matter the price now, we will pay later and with high interest. Nothing will save us from the consequences of our decisions at that moment; better a moment of shame than to live in pain.

There is no way to salvation if we let stereotypes mark us and impose on us their fashions and values. Even without agreeing, we can respect everyone without generating polemics or discussions that hurt. If they are wrong or we are, in the end, the consequences will make it clear who was wrong, and the consequences will react with the same force with which they were projected. However, it always seems to be greater than the action; the answer is easy because what we believe seems good is only a moment of wrong happiness. It usually vanishes, like water between the fingers, but when its consequence arrives, the clamoring and gnashing of teeth make a prey of pain and suffering. We think we do not deserve it, but there is the consequence: it comes directly to us or through others, hurting us and weighing us down. Instead, real happiness is that natural well-being that our nature claims, bringing a permanence that gives peace.

Many of us do not understand that pain is optional; I decide to bring it to my mind in the form of thoughts that hurt me at this moment; it is as if it had just happened that which has hurt us, without being able to flee from it. On the other hand, happiness lies within us naturally, only that we silence it with the voices that we give to our thoughts, those that cause us pain, and that many times we like to be there to condolence ourselves and thus carry the banner where others know the reasons that have prevented us from following, overcoming, or doing something different, that we have succumb. It is to want to take those poisons and have them hurt others.

An experience I received from my parents, always their opposites, was that my mother used to forgive everything; I never saw her hold a grudge, and she was quick to let things go, not so my father. He kept all the bad things about people in his heart, even if we were his own children and even if time passed. So always, in any conversation with anyone, he would bring out what the other person had done wrong, his defects, and worse, if they had bothered him or caused any harm to him, he would express comments that made you feel that you were the worst person that existed. You had to endure without interrupting; you could not; his imposition nullified you and exhausted your strength. You were left listening to everything he had to tell you. If it was to be put against, he knew how to do it very well too. By saying something bad from you to the others and from the others to you, it worked for him, all against all, without letting us create real bonds of the union as my mother tried to do, but our nature genetically predominated towards him for that part, and even as adults we could not be united.

It was so systematic that it seriously affected our relationships as siblings, where there was always a comment that kept us apart; that of divide and conquer always worked for him. Even though my mother, through her example, never managed to unite us, even after the deaths of both, we are still in that dilemma that has overcome us and with which I struggle so that my children and their children can get out of their lives forever. However, its power is sometimes already genetic, and we have to be in constant struggle.

They were nine siblings, six men and three women, all like us: very disunited, in constant competition, and concerned with appearances. There was an experience that was the most told story of his life, the one that took him forever away from his siblings; this tactic was with everyone, not just us, my mother, and his family; he did it with everyone he could, truly believing that he was right about everything. As a child, he knew how to face great calamities and believed in the help and cooperation between siblings; that trust goes beyond a signed paper; it is the word in between and even more so in those times when it was worth more than a paper, and even more so between siblings, who carry the same blood.

I do not know very well what happened, but what I remember is that when he arrived in the city, he looked for a way to get ahead and help his family; the two older ones did not care, so he took seriously his responsibility to help and provide at home (of which I can feel very proud to say that we loved him for things like that; he was an excellent provider and a hard worker; he had many good things), and this made him take advantage of all the opportunities that came his way. He knew how to save; both he and my mother were good at saving and making their savings and generating money. So the second of his older brothers knew that he had saved money and told him about a business that he knew would be attractive to my father, who fell into his nets and did the company, he swindled him, my father got upset, depressed, talked to his parents, brothers, and sisters but no one could do anything, over the years both went on with their lives, and my uncle came back to look for him, knowing that he had his savings, this long before I was born, Before he even met my mother, and to everyone's surprise, he was able to tell her another story where he appealed to her forgiveness and a new opportunity so that she would give him back what my father had done for him. In this situation, more people got involved who appealed to his good heart, and he fell again and exactly the same thing happened again, different situations, same result. This attacked my father in an atrocious way; it was fury at the beginning when he told this, then anger, frustration, and ending with that everything is paid, and hopefully he will not pay for what he has done

This led him to travel more, and on one of those trips, he met my mom, and they began a relationship that would mark their lives and allow us to have them as parents. This story stayed with him all the years of his life and marked him significantly; he was a good person, with very beautiful things that would make a separate list. Unfortunately, his personality was always tarnished by his mistrust, his anger, his jealousy, and his bitterness, and not only about us; he did it about everyone who approached him, always with some truth and wisdom in his words but in the end with pain and a lot of stored anger that used to always appear without ever letting it go in his life.

For years and years, he kept this story as his banner where he warned others about my uncle; he took so much poison that in the end, it hurt him the most, and with him we, his children, my mother, the women who loved him, and he never allowed a healthy relationship with anyone and that no one could trust since there would always be a latent uncle Aniceto who would abuse and defraud our trust. Not only my mother, his brothers, and a sister to whom he was very attached tried to persuade him. He said: "When it has happened to you and you have lost not only the money but also your confidence and security, then talk; only then will you understand what I went through."

His poison was acting in him, and I don't know if my uncle at some point was affected by this feeling my father had towards him or if he was ashamed of his dishonesty and wrongdoing with his brother; we were never close, and I could never even say that there could have been an interaction with him or his family, so I stay away from the other side and their version.

To act this way is to take the poison ourselves and wait for the other to die, to let it affect us, hurt us, and undermine our strengths, capabilities, and abilities to let it go and move on, being better at living the experience; if he hadn't had it, it wouldn't have happened to him.

Learning is difficult to do through others; we like to experiment in our own heads. It is said that the human being is the only animal that likes to stumble over a stone and repeat. I usually feel that inside us there is that little voice that activates our common sense, the least common of our senses, and warns us of situations that can harm us. Still, we live in such a way that external noises and mental justifications prevent us from listening to it, just like our bodies speak to us through sensations or pains that warn us that something is wrong. We still do not pay much attention to this divine communication with ourselves, and we insist on giving cheap excuses to express that we do not listen to them.

The hustle and bustle of our lives are already complicated; now imagine that we are stopped by something that warns us or tells us that something is not right. It is like stopping a downhill race suddenly; we believe that it will make us lose pace or that we are wrong, that our inner self does not know what our outer self is experiencing.

Although we have learned many things from others, there is something inside us that always tries to keep us safe and warns us that it is not good and that we are in danger; the only problem is that as we grow older, we stop paying much attention to it. We are silent with the noise presented on the outside; we resort more to the danger for the adrenaline that this implies. And then we ask ourselves, Why does it happen to me? As Albert Einstein would say, it is doing the same thing while expecting different results. And we can't; we must accept our consequences; there are limits to everything. To imagine going through life-destroying cars without believing that we will ever get hurt is like playing Russian roulette and hoping that the gun will never go off and cause us harm; it is to be prisoners of speed and hope that nothing ever happens to us, forgetting that accidents do happen.

However, we are desperately trying to adapt, survive, and keep ourselves safe, so evolution has helped us by inventing a feeling that allows us to have closer ties with others, where we can find bonds of love with others in different ways. How can we define love? Love is an invention of evolution that helps us to create close ties with other people, where we enter into sentimental synchrony, where I am emotionally synchronized with you and your emotions. If you suffer, I suffer with you. If you are happy, I am happy with you. It is a clean, healthy feeling.

This differs from empathy, which is an aspect of emotional intelligence, where a person with great empathy captures the emotions felt by others but does not feel them; I can perceive the emotions or feelings of others, but I do not feel them. There are no nuances between loving and wanting; they are opposites. Since love is to seek the good of others with sincerity of heart and feel what others feel, which differs tremendously from wanting, we can define it with expressions such as I want you for me, I'm fine if I have you, you belong to me, and "I belong to you, where there is possession without freedom and which can cause situations that put the integrity of people at risk. These limits speak of selfishness, blackmail, manipulation, and control of another; love, on the other hand, leads us to emotional synchrony that is in solidarity with others, seeks security and cooperation, and dramatically influences health.

On the other hand, in falling in love, there is passion and attraction to others with an ideological basis of desires, where we desperately seek the other with the objective of feeling pleasure beyond the sexual, where the circle of reward is activated, the closeness of the other person, a call, a text message, details that produce a feeling that overflows our enthusiasm. In its generality, it is very intense but very ephemeral, and it is perceived in our biological constitution as a drug, an addiction, or an addictive activity that activates the same neuronal circuits. When something that generates pleasure is produced, some nuclei are activated that have large amounts of hormones that generate chemicals that our brain perceives, interprets, and experiences as pleasure. We can reach a point where we experience a distortion of reality; we do not see reality objectively. The good thing is that it is not lasting; it is short-lived. Otherwise, it would cause severe damage to our health; we could not endure this emotion for long, much less with this intensity, where we are in a state of transient alienation.

It does not last for long and receives small doses of tranquility as caresses and looks that the other person gives as rewards that help us to continue in that situation; otherwise, like any addiction, if we do not have those stimuli, there is decay, anguish, or anxiety, where a breakup usually causes in both, in one more than another, the feeling of abstinence that makes us miss the habits that have been generated during the relationship. Missing their presence produces a state that is commonly called "lovesickness," which creates a psychological and physical condition that can lead to clinical depression. However, it depends on the personality of each one, and in extreme cases of vulnerability, they may need medical or psychiatric help with therapy and medication. Among its benefits, it could be said that falling in love is a powerful anti-stress treatment that helps us lower stress hormones such as dopamine and endorphins, leaving us relaxed. It helps to set goals and create new projects and illusions to pursue.

> "One should always be in love; we should never get married."
>
> Oscar Wilde

Being in love makes us give a more productive meaning to our existence; it achieves that thoughts generate feelings that allow us to have attachments, and bonds with other people, which make us generate love. This bond with others that makes us feel that madness that embraces us is very good, as it helps us develop independence with ties that unite us and fill us with passion. It is that feeling of pleasure that leads us to what we like or need, like water when we are thirsty or food when we are hungry. They come with pleasure and displeasure, what we like and dislike, what we enjoy and what we do not enjoy, making us more pleasurable in the company of others or in coexistence with others, and identifying our own ways of feeling good.

The ties and connections with all beings, where we can feel compassion, charity, forgiveness, love, empathy, and all those feelings that bring out the best in us, that help us overcome the past, giving space to the present, to live truly enjoying what we have here and now, to feel that everything has a reason to be, and what is not also has its foundation, that action produces a consequence that can benefit us if we are doing the right thing, and that this, in the end, will prod

Realize that emotion is short-lived and that we can learn to manage it, that abuse, disappointment, mockery, or shame, including revenge, are situations that we must not engage in, and that we can be susceptible to them if we do not define our position before them. For other people who want to inflict some pain on us or who, in their ignorance, are looking for someone to take out their frustrations on, we can understand that giving them the power is to stop being the ones in control. Even in more extreme cases, allowing our minds to be controlled by ourselves is giving us the opportunity to set limits on the frequency or intensity of the damage. If we achieve that, we will know how to handle ourselves without the outside affecting our inner selves.

Yes! We are crazy because we are learning to kill that being that others have invented and that has gone through life pretending to be someone who is not. They punish us with contempt and ignore us; they kill us in their lives, not ours. The madman must die; who is that madman? Is it me, or is it you, who has more madness? Those of us who believe that change is worth changing or those who believe there is no other way but to pretend

The madman who must die is because he does not adapt to what is marked, he does not submit to the rules, he differs from the laws and acts by himself, he asks everything, and he wants answers. To that madman, we must make him pay, hurt him, see him dwarfed, minimize him, lest others rebel and discover, invent, or do more things that serve humanity.

Yes, I am crazy; we all are, each in his own way; no one is equal to another. It is this blessed madness that allows us to feel the sun on our faces, to see life through the eyes of a child, and to eat when we are hungry, and not because it is time to eat. It is young people of advanced age who usually enjoy life, not seventeen-year-olds who are bitter without being able to be happy.

It is to do crazy things and let yourself be carried away by the present moment in all its fullness, to get wet in the rain, to eat with hunger or with your hands, to stay in the grass watching the clouds go by, to play ball, to be happy doing what we do, to love without conditions and without expecting anything in return, to take off our masks and bless the thieves because this has allowed us to let the sun touch our faces, not allow us to see life in our own way and that what has been taken from us does us better than harm. And if they wish, they can keep them, for they are of no more use to us; we no longer need them. We are free from everything and everyone. We were born to be happy and to see life with our own eyes, to choose freely as long as we choose between the good, the best, or the excellent without staying with the broken record in our minds that do not let us move forward.

There are no justifications; time brings us closer and closer to our hour; we should not fear; on the contrary, living to the fullest will help us to accept that moment and that the people we love remain in peace, accepting it too. Death cannot hurt us if we do not know what is next. It is only to progress and continue; our energy is charged with what we want to take. It is our obligation to know how to select what we will take to the hereafter, the universe of our creation, where our light will shine like the stars illuminating, sharing with all that once crossed our lives; it will be the way to be grateful for everything we have, everything we have lived, and the reason must always have that comfort of having recognized all the love that is within us, all the love that we could generate both in us and in others.

The madman must die; I don't think so; we must let him live so that he can change the world, discover something, invent something, create something that makes the general conscience respect the individuality and uniqueness of each one, and what if that madman is me?

"Wisdom comes through lack of experience."

CHAPTER IV
BUILDING A LIFE

The more you know yourself, the more clarity there is.

Self-knowledge has no end.

You don't come to an achievement, you don't come to a conclusion. It is an endless river.

Krishnamurti

"The worst hurts we tend to go through in our lives most often come from those we love the most."

Once, a person that I never thought could help me in any way, much less overcome the damage inside me—a being even more damaged than me—helped me realize that not everything is completely bad, nor is it completely good. It often goes between light and dark without always staying as one. I learned with him, in every talk, that every event has a reason for being, and we are the ones who can change its meaning if we want to. It is like putting a shield in front of us that dodges poisoned arrows that others throw at us, and even if they touch us, we can evade the damage and overcome it. In that conversation, we concluded that we are so used to seeing the black spot on the white dress that we stop perceiving it as more white than black; that little spot, no matter how small it is, can end up ruining the whole dress if it is not controlled.

I talked with him about the universe, creation, God, evil, love, money, plants, animals, science, technology, and famous people who discovered something. Regarding other topics, we were different. He liked technology, programming, robotics, computer science, and creating engines; we even thought of making a car with a water engine. We were good at creating and devising. They were dreams that came up in our conversations. For me, to see how to earn more by working less,

One day, a close relative of mine, a woman who worked one shift, earned very little a week; I asked her: "What should you do to earn more? The following week she told me: "I already know what I have to do to earn twice as much: work another shift." Then I looked at her and said, "And to earn triple?" I did not get an answer, and I did not expect it. She had started a business before. She left it when it began to be productive; she told me it was because it was a lot of work and responsibility.

This did not happen with my brother, but he had his vices; for me, that was enough of a commitment. Life distanced us a little, but from time to time, we would coincide again with a phone call and conversations that never ended.

A person who had such opposite extremes with a thirst for learning is very similar to mine: a being who fell into wrong decisions that gave him a bad reputation for bad actions. Someone who, like me, experienced things similar to mine but perceived them in his own way. He was my older brother, and like all of us, we were somehow fractured into many pieces that, through time, we have tried to put together. Looking for the way they can make us work with those pieces, we seek to be better people. However, circumstances have not allowed us to choose which parts of those pieces we want, making mistakes that present themselves as voices from the past reliving the damages again, bringing suffering again as if it had just happened.

From a very young age, he learned to be subjected to moments that made him suffer the mistreatment our father presented in the house. And regardless of his young age, his parents forced him to do things to become a tough, macho, strong man. His life transcended in that way until he had the opportunity to change and to love himself as he was, and suddenly time ran out.

It was not very often that my father was at home, so the events were not constant but very cruel. The frequency disappeared along with the intensity.

At that time, video games were not so common. In fact, people paid him to make it popular since others did not know how to play it. He enjoyed playing with the little machines they put in the stores. In his time, the games we usually had at home were not as standard as now; they were boxes with monochromatic monitors and levers, without slots, so they were turned on or off directly, so the owners of the store controlled their operation, connecting them when they were paid two pesos, and that lasted until the player lost; you could not play again until you disconnected and reconnected the machine; you had to pay again. The funny thing about this is that he could play for hours without losing his three lives that the game gave by default; there were lines of children waiting for him to lose to have his chance to play; there were times when the owner did not know how to tell him that he was losing money to be there playing, but in his face you could see the enthusiasm; There were times when the owner did not know how to tell him that he was losing money playing, but in his face you could see the enthusiasm, so they opted to leave him; other times they did not let him play because they knew that if he started, hours could pass without him losing, in which many times it was more the tiredness that stopped him; seeing him there escaping from his reality was common; so much time passed until our mother went for him because he did not pay attention, neither hunger nor thirst made him stop. This lasted all through high school, where he became skilled in other things, such as bodybuilding and vegetarianism. He learned to repair any device that came into his hands.

I cannot say now that he made many mistakes; I am not the person to say it, and if he did, I think he should be forgiven. Because when you are a child, you usually repeat what you are taught, and curiosity is only to see what it feels like to perform what you are taught or what you are forced to learn or perform. If he did not do it, he used his body to receive all kinds of aggression that I find hard to understand. My father carried his idea of making him a man, another macho like him, by exposing him to situations where his time of play and fun was exchanged for moments of repression and aggression. In the separation that we lived with my parents, he benefited, and in his adolescence, he could have some peace. He tried to heal himself and looked for a family that helped him, feeling the responsibility that led him to provide in his home. That game that helped him escape from reality was the same one that allowed him to generate a company that helped him do many things.

He designed video game machines and even slot machines. He built the furniture, adapted screens, buttons, levers, slot machines, regulators, their power cables, and controls, and made routes where he placed them in businesses. He sold them and also repaired them. Those were years that made him focus on the work that allowed him to help others. He paid for one of his nephew's schools, and he gave work to several people until everything came to an end. Our mother died, who was his greatest love, and for her, he confronted our father so he would never attack her again. My father began to whisper his fears to a sister who worked with him; he made her believe he was his son because of her. She was gullible and believed it, and she ended up leaving him. They lasted more than a decade together, making an excellent, successful team built on mutual trust.

She managed, and he created. She lost control of reality, and she believed the only words of someone who, out of ignorance or envy, wanted to defeat him. They separated and he continued, but that crime put him on several tests that took the lives of people he loved, workers, and friends who started this dream with him. The first time he did not let himself be intimidated; a second time, and the third time he could not resist any longer and left for another place. He put land in the middle, which also ended in the separation of his family; his children stayed with him, so he was mom and dad. Unfortunately, in those moments, that little boy came out again with fears; he relived his traumas and doubts again. Although, economically, he could live like that for almost another ten years without having to work, he only controlled his business from a distance. Like everything else, the passage of time was gradually diminishing his resources. Although he always undertook something with his vision, the world was not close to him until he reached a point where he got into a whirlwind of storms that began to hit him mercilessly, between bad friendships and people who think differently.

I must say that we were never very close. I do not know if we were different or the same; we did not know how to have a close relationship. The few times we talked or met evidenced our opposite ways of seeing things; we did not understand each other, plus the distance and different ways of life made for a very dry relationship, but he helped me at some point. I helped him at another time, but it did not go further. However, as much as I tried to dissuade my sister that I was fine with him, I failed.

Going to his house on New Year's Eve and spending time with him left me with a lesson I learned from him, which always encourages me to believe in people. I can say that he was an excellent cook; for New Year's, he used to make lobster tails that fascinated me, so he used to tell me: "There will be lobster tails for New Year's dinner. You are invited", so I knew perfectly well that I would go with my whole family. The last New Year's Eve dinner that we were together, we arrived at his house, as usual, ready for dinner. The dishes were served, and the first thing that was finished was the lobster. His wife, at that moment, took the last dish and looked at me, saying: "There is no more, sorry sister-in-law. When he realized this situation, he took the plate he had in his hands and had already started to eat and gave it to me, licking his fingers and saying, "Eat it; tomorrow I will make more. We said no more words, and the night passed, and that action made me see a glow of kindness inside him, which never disappeared from my mind. Whenever I got angry with him for something or wanted to hang him figuratively, I thought that behind his erratic decisions and actions was a being to rescue, a child disguised as an adult with good things inside him.

How do you help someone who does not want to be helped? What is greater, and what is stronger? I did not think that the one who needed help was me. Sometimes to see others who are wrong is to realize the mistakes, and if we realize the mistakes, those who are wrong are us because to realize is to perceive what can hurt, so being in that consciousness makes us responsible for our actions. They have not learned and, in their ignorance, do not know what they do wrong. Some even create addictions to justify their actions—one or two drinks just to get courage—and then, in the raw, it is so simple to say that I do not remember and so forget everything, but I am not forgiven, as it continues to damage those who live it.

We lived through something similar. Just a couple of years before, we had to change cities. We lost a lot of stability and separation, so I tried to tell him what would happen if he was not cautious. I could not speak in the same tone, and relationships, wrongs, abuse, and addictions led him to hit rock bottom. He asked for my help, and I helped him, and that caused me to be in a situation that made me hate him the moment I found out, but always believing that we can overcome everything, I let life go on.

We began communicating for things that life provided, and I only listened to him, even though my children do not believe it. I was tired of giving him advice or giving my opinion about the life of someone older than me. We started to communicate more often, and as if I were his therapist, he talked to me about what he was living; I asked him, Are you okay? How do you feel? What do you think, what is it good for, and how will you make it? A very special person began to emerge. Although certain misgivings made me lose confidence in him sometimes, I felt that the phone was safe between us. It did not make us live together, causing damage. It was volatile and neurotic; maybe he was looking at me in a mirror. "What shocks you, shocks you," and I started, thanks to him, to change, to try to be a better person. I saw myself with my own demons, fears, and traumas. Ultimately, we had lived almost the same, but in a different way, with our same fears and traumas.

Talking about what we had lived through was painful, something in our minds resisted seeing the reality, but that made us overcome it, to know that it was past, that it should stay there, that our mind loves sad stories, that our ego wants to say that we are the ones who have suffered the most, but when two people see the story from different points of view, we can realize all the damage we went through, and through those conversations, my dramatic picture can be realized.

As time went by, I realized that he was struggling with alcohol and some pills; I didn't know what else he was struggling with, and I didn't want to ask him either. I feared that fact since I am usually a person who, by my own decision, decides not to drink or smoke. Until I was 33 years old, I didn't say a bad word and tried to be good. However, I didn't perceive myself that way until a doctor came to me and said, "Sorry, I did not understand what he meant, so I made an appointment with him. He told me the marks on my face were chemical reactions that my liver was discharging because of what I was carrying. He sent me homeopathy to help me a little, but the real cure depended on me; only by releasing my burdens would I free my body. I worked on it until I got over it, and those talks did me a lot of good. There was someone like me who had suffered in a similar way and in the same place, only in a different way and with a different point of view of the situations that arose there".

We tend to think that everyone else is fine, that they go through life so safely and perfectly that we are ashamed even to express our fears and sorrows. We believe that we are exclusive of pain. It is not so; everyone carries their own events that have somehow marked some insecurity, fear, pain, or shame that has lodged inside us, leaving burdens that do not allow us to be us in reality, so our lives become like a puzzle that we must put together with the pieces that we have from our exhausted bodies, minds, and spirits, situations that have taken us to the limit, and that many of us have taken the habit of repeating or looking for escapes that make us absent ourselves from reality, which does not allow us to bring to our minds those experiences.

Our relationship was very intermittent until he suddenly behaved like a small child, to whom I had to demand that I take the reins of his life. To overcome everything and that if he had succeeded once, he could do it again and better, that with his experience and skills, it was only a matter of deciding. He called me one day and told me he was in love. He went to another state and got married; it was so fast. For me, it was just wishing him the best since, from that talk with the doctor, I understood that I could repeat the story of my father with his brother and stay in that same situation, harboring hatred and resentment that would not lead me to any suitable place or path.

As time went by, he began to have problems. He began to run out of money from his business and had to start working. At his age and without the preparation required, he began to suffer more and more until he fell into addictions, sleeping pills, which were not welcomed by his wife, and I think by anyone you want to see well. There came a time when he called me on the phone and told me that he had fallen twice and that his head hurt a lot. I was driving to a meeting I had scheduled, so I said to him that as soon as I got out, I would call him. Before going in, I dialed him to know if he was okay, to which he responded: "I am hungry. "That expression puzzled me a lot. I could not be concentrated in my meeting because of those words. When I asked him, "I am hungry. " She responded with complaints and examples of situations with problems that did not interest me. I repeated the question, and she told me that he was not there, so I told her that something was not right and that I had anxieties (which are sensations that take over my interior as if warning something, and so I usually call them), so she went to her house, I redialed her, and she told me between shouts: "Your brother is dead."

I was speechless; the words were silenced in my mouth, and my eyes accumulated tears about to burst. I heard the paramedics arrive, and he hung up on me. I waited for some news. He dialed me after about ten minutes and told me that they had done CPR and that he was alive and that they were going to the hospital. From there, he redialed me and told me that my brother had gone into a coma. I started to cry. The next day, my son and I went to see him. We arrived at the hospital, and I went to see him. He was so swollen that it looked like he could explode at any moment. With devices everywhere and calls from many people who had already found out, his wife said he would not make it through the night. I resigned myself to that situation. At fifty years old, I thought he was too young to end his life. She left me with him to go home to get some rest. At that moment, the doctors came and talked among themselves about a suicide attempt.

I approached them and told them that this was not correct, and if it was right to tell me what medications to call the doctors for, I knew to tell me what was going on. They replied that his wife had told him he had tried to commit suicide. I said no, that he had fallen twice and hit his head, as he had told me. Hence, the day before, a doctor sent him for a CT scan, and it turned out that his brain was very swollen, so much so that they changed the medications. In moments, it began to deflate, his face began to look more normal, and you could see one of the blows on his head. His wife, when she returned, could not believe what was happening. She had already resigned herself to another outcome. I saw so many people arrive from both sides that as soon as he opened his eyes and saw me, I kissed him on his forehead, let him know how much I loved him, and said a prayer with him. We retired to rest. The next day, with his children and grandchildren there and the family that would go to see him, I decided that my work was over. We returned home, and on the way, I was praying for him that God would allow him to go well, enjoying a little more of life.

He was released and managed to get out in less than a week. When he was discharged, he was taken to another hospital, where they usually put people who are not well in their mental faculties and do not allow anyone to have contact with them; only direct family members can visit. He was isolated for several weeks; I could only hear from him through his wife—not a call or message. I only knew what she told me. As time passed, she maintained her position that my brother had wanted to commit suicide. Then, if his life was in danger, maybe she could do something for him, and she told me that she did not want him in her house. I told her there was no problem and that as soon as she knew when he would be discharged, she should talk to me, and I would go for him.

One Sunday, without preamble, she called me and told me that they were discharging my brother at that moment and that I should go get him; by road, it was many hours. It was already late by plane; the flights to that place were not very frequent, so I told her not to worry and that I would talk to Armando and fix the situation. I was thinking of paying for a hotel for him to spend the night in and sending him a ticket to come to my house. I couldn't make it, and I couldn't talk to him. She told me that my brother had left and wasn't coming back. I got scared; then I started to receive strange messages from her. I want to think that it was her desperation for everything she had lived through.

The next morning, with many messages sent, I finally received the long-awaited call from my brother. I heard his voice, and I felt it was someone else—very serene, changed—and he told me to go and pick him up at the head office. That was all; not another word was said.

I picked him up. I was so happy to see him; he was my brother, after all, and blood calls. It is only in ourselves that we can forget the bad we have lived and allow ourselves to see the good that someone, no matter how bad it may seem, always has. I hugged him, and he told me that as soon as he left the hospital, he felt like a mangy dog and that he was not welcome in that place, so he went to a park and spent the night there, saying that he preferred the cold of the night and the insecurity to knowing that he was not welcome in a place. I usually think that way.

He stayed only one night at my house, and we put him on the first flight back with his children. At first, he didn't want to, but he had to face his fears; besides, children and grandchildren are usually a balm for everyone. He told me that in that place, he was everything he learned, and when he left, his abstinence made him control his dependence on his addictions. He could see himself better than he was and understand that there was always an opportunity to move forward and that it was his time to do it.

He was a different person, and his insecurities began to give way. He became productive, he began to dream, we coincided with business without having another income, he got busy, and he became active. We did and planned business in the administrative and economic resources areas. He is in charge of the development and production, first selling caps and cell phone cases, which were not very good, then a line of sauces that he developed completely from the recipe to its production and packaging. We did well, but not as well as we wanted. Then, among other things he did, we started to develop a CNC, a numerical control machine that he was designed to cut from paper to granite; at the same time, he began to learn how to lay wiring for Wi-Fi networks, and he told me, "If I learn well, we can start a company that takes routes, we get contracts from the big companies, we buy a fleet of small trucks, we prepare the personnel, I manage, you manage."

He fell off a ladder, dialed me, and in his joking tone, told me, "You almost had coffee on my own", a term used for funerals. He told me how it was; I was worried, and he was worried that nothing would happen to me. He had fallen from a ladder almost four meters high. A month passed, and he began to have pains. He told me that he had gone to the doctor and that his spine had shrunk a few centimeters. He said to me that I had become shorter, still in his joking tone, thinking that nothing was wrong with him. He survived the pandemic but could not survive the fall. Before this happened, he met a woman who loved him for the first time. You may wonder why I say that. Simple: only love does things that make us better people, motivate us, and help us overcome everything.

He became someone else; he changed radically, leaving his bitter experiences behind. He resurfaced a better person, with optimism and without fear, to look again for a path that would allow him to overcome as he wanted. By his side, someone special to live everything with, with whom to share without arguments or problems that would cause some regret or disappointment. He expressed himself so beautifully about her; he wanted to put the world at her feet. This fact made me love her too and be grateful for the opportunities that life was giving him, not only to him but also to his children, since she is still watching over them as if she were their own mother. One day he called me, as was customary for us, and told me that he was going to the doctor for a check-up. Then he called me again and told me that he was going to have other tests because it was hard for him to breathe. Time passed, and I went to rest. I was dreaming about him, and he did not say a word to me. He was only in a tunnel of light that let me see his silhouette and a raised hand, saying goodbye; then my phone rang, and without thinking, I said, "Did he die? I don't remember if it was his wife or his daughter; they only affirmed that yes, he had left two weeks before his fifty-fifth birthday, on the eve of Christmas, when all the children were waiting for him to be present. I received this terrifying news, which I still find hard to talk about without shedding a tear or two.

I received as many condolences calls as stories about him. A cousin told me that one day when he was training in bodybuilding or weightlifting, he lifted weights on his own just to show off his strength. A friend told me he loved talking to him because he always took life as a game filled with laughter and jokes. One more person told me that he never really understood that he played and joked about hiding his sorrows, but that his intelligence used to play tricks on him and that he was a good friend. A friend told me that, as well as being handsome, intelligent, and a good person, God would put a star next to my dad and mom and that, from heaven, he would illuminate my dark nights.

I usually look at the sky and try to guess which star is his; although I usually talk to all of them and express my gratitude, thanks to him and my children, I was able to understand that everything we lived as children left strong, good people who never stopped being children. Despite the years, or as my oldest daughter told me, "You are not getting older, you are just getting younger," and it is true, that applied to him too; to all of us, we feel that we are made of plastic, that we can do anything. There are limits that we lose sight of; our fears have been so hurt that we do not see the risks. We believe that nothing will happen to us; if it does, he is no longer here, like many to whom I have given pieces of my heart. I have already started to accumulate people in heaven, and there are more than I would like.

In the end, I was able to fix myself by getting to know him more. I healed my wounds, but I never told him. I usually think I am very strong; I lock myself in steel armor that does not let me project that I am sensitive and weak only so as not to let my weakness show. And that with him, I was able to put aside and start a new me again, putting pieces of my life together to create a new opportunity, like an endless puzzle that constantly changes images. It is not possible for me to finish.

I am very sorry that those who have known me in my effusive or expressive moments that have hurt cannot change another image of me. I did see the changes in him, and I hope others see them in me. It was so noticeable. Unfortunately, many of his mistakes marked people I love, and it hurts me to think that they are left with that bad image of him without his forgiveness, which frees not only them but also us from something terrible we may have done out of ignorance, wrongdoing, or repetition. EVERYTHING HAPPENS FOR SOMETHING, AND IT ALSO DOES NOT HAPPEN FOR SOMETHING. The reasons will always be the reasons for everything. What now may seem bad to us, in the end, will be the only thing that will make us understand that we can change and that there will always be a last chance waiting for us to take it and stop suffering.

To put together our lives with the pieces left of us, we must understand that they are the best parts of us, and that even among them, we can decide which parts we want to keep and which we don't. Breaking up has not been bad; on the contrary, it can remove from our lives what is not for us and what we don't want to have anymore.

Assembling a life is to make it better. It is to enjoy this opportunity, forgive, let go, and hope to continue.

A few days ago, I fell from a hammock. It was so fast that my husband got so scared that the pressure went down, I felt like my chest was on my face, and I was completely on the floor. Since I had studied first aid, the first thing I did was instinctively touch the back of my neck. They said that if you feel like marbles in a bag, it is not good to move, and you need to immobilize the neck immediately or wait for medical help. I thought I was fine, so I got up and tried to make my husband feel that nothing was wrong. When I saw his face, I knew it was not something simple that had happened to me. I took pain medicine, called my doctor, explained what happened, and he told me that if I had certain symptoms to go to the emergency room. But nothing like that happened. At night I had a dream in which I clearly heard my brother's voice telling me: "Take care of yourself; everything can happen because of a fall. See my example." I woke up crying and started praying. I miss him so much that I still find it hard to know he is gone. I am going to take better care of myself. I know that our bodies are very fragile; an accident can end our career in life sooner than expected, and we should not leave earlier than planned because there are still things to do, learn, and enjoy; hugs to give; love to spread; and kisses to give.

So, I take advantage of the time as much as I can, and I let everyone I care about know it, but more importantly to my children, I express to them that if I have made mistakes or oversights that have caused them some pain, that they should personate me, that they should overcome it, and that they should learn from it. May they not carry burdens that prevent them from seeing life as beautiful in the good expressions that it offers us and all that we can enjoy.

Let us avoid leaving so many dreams, illusions, goals, words, and actions in a pause that will never be carried out again.

Today I learned that:

"Life is a terminal disease.

—That there is nothing more dangerous than death!

"That life is a deadly disease, which ends with the death of the individual!

So, to worry about what is real, let us leave the past dead and buried, without chasing the future and always running after it. No matter how fast we want to be, we will never reach it. Better let us live God's present, blessed gift, trying to be better every day, and imagine better "how we want to be remembered!"

This will be our task.

BROKEN DOLLS

To stop time is not enough today. To go back a nd stop those moments where we are you and me against the world, full of dreams, ambitions, and projects that remain silent with your departure. The love between us does not die, but you leave me, like many others before you, and you find that eternal progress where I still can't be. To stop in the mind's moments, I miss and fade with time as fast as the race of life advances, and always, in the end, there will be death. Physical, earthly, and material death, where my eyes will no longer be able to contemplate the faces of those who possess my heart. They become a memory that is stored in my mind like so many others.

The most joyful moments of my life have been filled with wonderful beings, and just as some arrive, are born, and develop, others succumb to their eternal moment to follow; today it was your turn, tomorrow it will be mine, and today it is my turn to cry for you. It comforts me to know that my parents did not live through your departure, and with open arms, they showed you the way to eternity.

I love you as I have loved few people in my life, and like you, they left a mark on my soul and a hole in my heart, tearing a piece when leaving. I keep the love of those I now have because if I did not have them, I would run after you, not letting you go alone, taking your hand, and staying together in eternity.

The promises, the projects remain: silence, a cruel silence where there will be no more echoes of your voice on the other side of the line.

Death is that small instant where the idea and the reason hang by a thread, where madness and pain become present with desperation. It is there that we can understand everything that can miss someone. It is that moment where the "would have" remains and the words are silenced, oppressing the chest to such a degree that it is impossible to breathe. The screams of pain and crying take over in silence for some or in thunderous cries for others.

To lament death is to feel how we follow paths beyond this world, where faith gives us a little peace; to think of resurrection, of eternal progress, the energy that belongs to us is not destroyed but transformed into continuous improvement. It gives a little peace to our souls.

Each being that departs takes a little of my reason, of my understanding, of me. Knowing that we are going to die is not the same as losing someone; understanding that death is for everyone is not the same as seeing how others leave and fill a part of our days with darkness.

I immerse myself in myself and embrace myself, allowing myself to be carried away by the love of each memory that forms my happiness, where there are all those I love, have loved, and will love, good moments or bad, I prefer not to have lived them, there are no hatreds, only changes of direction to calm the moment, although these moments sometimes last longer than they should, there is no anger, only different perspectives on the same situation, there are no discussions, only moans,

Your light went out so soon. You left empty a part of my life—the one where a message made my day. I rescued you once; twice I couldn't, and not knowing your path was so short, I would have walked by your side without losing a moment; even without shoes and with bare feet, I would have done it, even bleeding my feet. I wouldn't have allowed myself to miss a moment by your side. I say this by way of apology because this part I also have is that we want to return that time that was lost in time. Even being my older brother, you were always like a little boy. You never lost that childish part in you, and although life hit you in every possible way, you always kept that part that helped you to believe again; I know you hurt. Still, it was because of your upbringing and your ignorance, because no other way was known. We lacked games and fun, because life did not let us remain children, and we had to grow up and face life, where a broken doll remains a toy in the eyes of a boy or a girl.

I remember you with pains, with problems, with joy, with happiness, in the games, in the fights. All memories are worth keeping. I want to miss you; for me, those are moments when we are together, when I am with you, when you hug me, when I do not leave you alone. I know that in an oversight, I lose you; you see, that oversight came and took you farther away from me than a distance allows me to reach.

Like today, there have been other moments where my pain is similar and I see your faces, and that makes me very happy! I don't want the darkness of oblivion to extinguish them; I want them to last beyond my life, reach my mind, and change my attitude.

Death dressed in sackcloth covers my head; my tears do not stop flowing; my memories accumulate in my mind; I see your images; and my throat has lost its voice at times.

I love you, and my love goes beyond this silence that you leave. My love follows you wherever you go, blesses you, and thanks you for what you did for me and your help. Because in the end, we knew how to be brothers, I recognize your intelligence and ability to always get ahead, and I know that there were moments when you almost lost yourself; I almost lost you. In the end, you overcame all; you overcame your fears, your traumas, the bad people, and it was you, happy and full of happiness, that in the end saw you leave as the best of all, the best brother, son, father, grandfather, and companion. Now you leave me orphaned without you—first my grandparents, then my daughter, then my parents, then my teacher, and now you. I pray for your soul and your energy to transcend, to not forget me, and to help me feel that you are well. And to be children again, ignoring the worries of adult people, the work, the illness, and the pressures of life that leave us tired. To play with those broken dolls that still have room in their broken bodies, to make them clothes as you taught me, and to cover their battered bodies not only with new clothes made of scraps but also with other eyes, Those who see a doll to play with and who become princesses in castles waiting for their prince charming with broken dolls gave me the chance to know that no matter how broken they were, it was our eyes that looked at them beautifully.

I love you, and this does not change. It hurts, and I know this pain will stop at some point. For now, only rest and sleep make me feel at peace. In them, I try to dream of you, to see your face again, even without saying a word, and to see you happy.

To my brother Armando

CHAPTER V
THE LAST MEXICAN MACHO

I'm starting to pay! Better to start early, to finish early.

Pedro Paramo, by Juan Rulfo

In a place with a cold climate, at the coldest time of the year, he was born in a ranch family, near the city, far from the civilization of that time, where he knew from a very young age how to learn how to survive. He liked the countryside; he used to tell adventures that brought him good moments, with which he disguised the reality that hurt him. He was the third son of the marriage, all men, the pride of those for the father of the family, in times where this used to mean how macho he was when painting pure men, or mostly, since he had three women and six men, being nine in total.

Taken to register by a neighbor of the place and to bear the name Amando, he grew up in a way that gave him a personality very much his own, although it marked like hot iron his macho mentality that prevailed until the last days of his life.

The absence of his father forced him to travel to the capital. His mother had no choice but to look for him in the capital, and they had to leave the little they had left behind.

They used to be one of the most prosperous in the region. Unfortunately, his father's bad administration and squandering forced them to make this trip without the slightest possibility of returning. Although he always harbored that hope, he never carried it out.

They left behind stories of success and sorrow that would take them from that place's tranquility to the city's turmoil. A little more than an hour away by car at this time, where roads and highways make it much easier to travel than before on dirt roads. Trucks stopped in each village, picking up and dropping off passengers, some in wagons or on horseback. From time to time, they achieved a real road that protected the travelers with its shadows flanked on both sides of the road by trees, exposing them to the dangers of the evildoers of the time. There were risks that had to be overcome, and in his comings and goings, he learned the safe way to return from time to time to that place that always called him and to which he never belonged again.

—Where are we going, mother?

—In search of your father, to have security, to follow life. To demand what your father took from us and to hold him accountable.

Words that brought no meaning, echoes that resonated all his life in him, and that, on the contrary, exposed him to more fears, unanswered questions, and exposure to an unknown adventure.

Then he asked his mother:

—Why look for him?

"Shouldn't he worry about being by our side and taking care of us? Taking care of his family?" he thought, without saying a word, leaving the place where he grew up in the distance.

A place where he saw the sun for the first time, where the fears of being that man his father wanted to bring him many misfortunes, fears, and insecurities that formed shadows throughout his life.

They used to have the best lands and houses in the region; they survived the revolution, being well off because of their relationships with the right people. His uncle Francisco used to say that everyone has a price; you just have to know how to reach them. So their ancestors knew how to leave a future for all their children, but not so for women. These usually depend on a man, who will be the one to provide what they need if they know how to choose.

So, when they married, the men received land, cattle, and houses on which they could work. In this way, they got ahead. Some were smarter than others; as far as can be deduced, his father was not very skilled in that aspect. He began to do business in the capital. Both the products of the land and those of the cattle began to produce a good economy. He and his brother managed to amass goods and fortunes that made them powerful.

Both had different and opposite ideas, and even though they were brothers, they ended up separating and living different lives. Uncle Francisco would remain all his life in his lands; he bought everything from his brother at low prices. He amassed his fortune at the cost of advantageous deals that he always knew how to take advantage of.

He used to say: "The hungrier you make someone go, the better price you will get.

They were tall, good-looking people, of pleasant aspects, of strong character, those that used to be called "machos." For them, it was to be men or not to have been born—prepared in the reasons of the field, the land, the people, the animals. Knowledgeable about the climate, rainy season crops, assiduous to strong drinks, and scratching the throat so that the body feels them Womanly and good in their own way.

No one can know the ways of others; there will always be reasons that usually justify their actions.

Don Margaro and Don Francisco saw life differently. One never left his land, stayed alone, and never gave in to anything. They were men who did not know how to give in.

For them, women were to be used and left, but not their wives, who, resigned, always had to accept their fragile condition as women and accept whatever they imposed on them, whether they liked it or not.

Don Francisco, for his part, was the lord and master of the place; as he kept everything he could, he knew that his dominion was great.

He used to ride on horseback. This made him look bigger than he was. Always with his horse, he went around the land, hurrying people without allowing them a break. That's why he paid them, he thought. His children, five in all, were four men and only one woman, who married when she was very young and was widowed without any help from him during her lifetime. The men emigrated to the capital; it is unknown if it was for the pleasure of going to study or fleeing from their personalities.

On the land, as was customary, there were little old houses far from the main one where the day laborers lived, buying everything on credit at the famous "tienda de Raya", the one that never let them be free of some extra income to dream of living somewhere else. Then the children ended up repeating the same story as their parents, enslaving their lives to what was available. Some escaped this and went in search of other directions. However, most could not. Their minds were stuck in what their parents and their parents' parents taught them. This is what you were born to do, and this is how you stay.

This is where the opportunities for abuse were created, where people became pack animals and not human beings who were given any consideration. The law was written by the owners, not the employees, who allowed everything and always kept quiet.

This terror reached the children among them, where they could be reprimanded for the simple fact of being adults and family, and woe to them if they were to gossip because they were doubly punished.

Amando used to say that his experiences were always bitter. On the one hand, he liked the idea of getting out of there and returning when he could buy what was theirs from his uncle Francisco (he never could; his dreams of being a rancher were suffocated in the end like his).

Uncle Francisco could take any woman, and at any time he wanted, he used to offend, hurt, and intimidate, with no other law than his own, so in the end, he died alone, in very unfortunate circumstances, and was hated by everyone in the region, who over the years began to break free from his yoke and abandoned him to his fate.

His children received the inheritance, and almost all of them wanted to get rid of the goods and distribute them. What were their reasons for not wanting to return to those lands? They had them. Only one saw an opportunity, and in his father's style, he kept everything, agreed on prices, looked for hunger among them, and did the operation.

In the excitement, he forgot his lack of experience in this new line of business, which was very different from what he decided to study and do in the city. Without giving it so much importance, he hired people who specialized in agriculture and filled the land with seeds and fruit trees. He bought machinery and all the necessary technology and transportation with this investment. He hoped that the harvest would make him prove that he was his father's son, and proud of this, he started his dream. He never imagined the fame that his father had. So he never expected the events that happened and the damage this would cause him. People never knew who he was, but they were happy to see all the things that began to happen: the crops dried up, and the fruit trees never bore fruit. He would think it was just a bad streak, and he tried again, now with the cattle—hundreds of heads of the best specimens, both for meat and breeding and for rent. The same thing happened—they all died little by little, without realizing it at first. One day, one or two The next day, as many others before it, the business was over again.

He started to sell; it was becoming a burden now, and no one wanted to buy. It was understandable. The townspeople said the land was cursed by the blood and pain his father caused, and they carried it in their heads too. Over time, few returned to that place. Abandoned lands await the moment to return to their moments of glory.

Margaro, for his part, began their relationship. At first, his first two children were happy; his first two children were boys, which made him more macho and helped men understand his nature. Pistols, horses, and work on the land—unfortunately for his wife, the years began to pass, and there was no more family, so he began to lose interest in his wife. Being wives only served to have a family; if they could not, they were burdens they did not want to bear. When the relationship had its problems, another son came into the world, Amando, whose name was not well known since in his birth certificate, it was clear the separation of the couple: "child born alive in the ranchera, presented by a neighbor of the place, he says that: due to problems in childbirth, he was sent to him to be baptized, lest he die and fall into limbo, that place where the innocent who never received the baptism go." In the end, everything went well, and soon another daughter arrived, the last one in that place.

Don Margaro began to spend more time in the capital, coming less and less to the family home. It was one of the best houses in the area because it was close to a river that always had water for the family's chores and to keep them clean. Cooks, maids, day laborers, and a caporal managed to keep up with and help the family in the absence of Don Margaro. He did not have such a bad reputation. In fact, it could be said that he lacked the character to be able to manage what he had inherited and that, in the end, he ended up losing everything.

In his comings and goings to the capital, he began to forget his duties as a father of a family. His presence should not only give them security but also teach them how to get ahead.

In his early years, Amando learned of the arrival of a teacher in the region, which made him very excited. He wanted to learn to read and write; although numbers were always his forte, it could be because of the need to count and weigh everything on the ranch. But his ability was incredible; he was a mental calculator that always had the right result. When she started going to school at that time, she had to bring her own wood and charcoal chalk to write with; there were no notebooks, and these had to be ordered from the capital. This did not matter to him, much less the abuse and bad temper of the teacher, who had to deal with so many students of different ages, some of whom were his older brothers. And no women, since school was not necessary for them. They had to work for their husbands and do the housework since they did not need to read or write, much less do accounts; that was for the men.

With his donkey corner, tables, chairs, and a blackboard, the classroom was an old house that her brothers, father, and uncle had given to her in order to educate these uninformed kids and help them better prepare themselves. One day, the teacher took one of his brothers by the ear, for some reason, and put him in the corner with the donkey ears, a fact that bothered him a lot and was made worse because he was one of the biggest in the classroom, so he went to complain to his father. Don Margaro, instead of understanding the event, beat him up for gossiping and not respecting an adult. As a result, Amanda never complained to him.

Since his older brothers were responsible for the house when Don Margaro was not there, the abuses began, and they took the same route, going to the capital to do business until they never returned to the ranch. Don Margaro only returned to sell, to fill his belly belts, those that you remove the buckle and you can put the silver or gold coins of those times and run less danger. Returning from time to time for more, they almost finished everything before leaving them in destitution and deciding to go to the capital.

When they arrived in the capital, they stayed in the center, near the cathedral and the government palace. What times were those when you could only find someone by asking? That happened, and they went to look for her father and brothers; among the crowds at that time, they found him, the father and husband. He was in a cantina with his friends, a place that decent women do not enter, so she and her sister waited outside. Amando was a boy, but his stature made him look older. He went into the bar, tapped him on the shoulder without making a noise to interrupt him, and when she saw him, she slapped him to the ground. Without saying anything, she left the place, and the message was clear: they had to wait and starve until he came out at night, drunk. They held him and went together to the hotel. There, they helped him lie down on the bed to rest. They went out to look for food; a quesadilla and tamale stand on the corner made them happy, and with their bellies full, they returned to rest.

The next morning their father woke up with the hangover from the day before. He took them to breakfast and took something for his hangover headache. They returned to the hotel; he paid for the room and gave his mother a silver coin to buy some things. They spent the whole day getting to know the *"zocalo"* of the city. There were many cars, trucks, and streetcars in which they could travel. They saw houses with so many patios that they used to be called *"vecindades del quinto patio",* which indicated the economic power of the people who lived there. The further away the house was, the cheaper it tended to be. There were always people coming and going, running all over the place.

The city had plenty of things to see and buy. When it was time for lunch, they went to a market and found a great variety of fruit. They knew some of them since the ranch used to eat what was produced in the area. Amando had his first encounter with the banana, and he fell in love with that fruit. It was love for life; he loved its flavor and even used to eat the peel. All his life, he was a good eater. People used to say when they saw him eating that the food was very good or he had gone days without eating. He enjoyed every bite, and when he finished, he always took his drink—never in between his meal, always at the end. He said he got more out of it that way. So you should always listen to your body; it speaks and tells you things. You just have to pay attention to it.

The day passed, and they returned to rest. Their father did not get to spend the night with them. The next day they were awakened by the knock on the door; it was their father, and they received him happily. Without showing any emotion, he told them:

—Prepare your things; we are leaving.

Immediately they took a cab that brought them to an unknown destination, far from where they were. As time went by, the houses and the well-built avenues were being left behind. They were beginning to enter less glamorous neighborhoods; the houses were simpler, but there was pavement. As time went by, there were only dirt streets. The houses were poorly built and built out of necessity and without form.

Suddenly, the car stopped. There was nothing beautiful in that place. It smelled of poverty and misery, usually associated with "poverty belts," places people look for to make irregular settlements where they can live. There was no water, electricity, or drainage. He stopped the car and left them in front of some poorly made rooms with a bathroom far from them. There was a water pump in the corner of the house and another one outside the house that provided water to the people of that place. They had water, which, for a person so fond of cleanliness, pleased him but not his mother, who saw that sad scenario with a face of disappointment. However, she said nothing about what she thought. On the contrary, she thanked her husband for helping them, imagining how she could fix that. Without saying a word, she took out another coin, gave it to him to buy what he needed, and took the cab back to the city, leaving them to their fate.

His mother moved and bought an oil stove, some beds, and curtains, among other things needed for her family, like laundry and food. They spent the night, and the days went by, not knowing when his father would come again, and money was getting scarce. Amando sat in the doorway, wondering, "What are we doing here?" He suddenly paid attention to the people lining up to get water and take it home in buckets. An idea came to him: take water to the houses! When it began to get dark, he armed himself with two buckets and a piece of wood that he placed as a "water carrier" so he could make more trips and not get so tired, he thought.

He spent the whole night doing this task, and he recognized his sad moments when he lost his fear of the night:

His father used to say that to become men, they should not be afraid of anything. So, after midnight, he used to call him and ask him to go to Uncle Francisco's house to ask for a cigarette. He could not refuse; he already knew the consequences of doing so, and there were no pleas from his mother because he would also receive his own. He would not lower him as a cowardly son of mommy, so he got up, took his hat, and went out in the middle of the night, under the thick darkness, waited for his eyes to get used to it, and started his way. There were nights when the beautiful moon took pity on that boy and gave him its light. He used to hear grunts, noises, and voices. He used to see figures and shadows that used the night to scare him even more. He would hurry his pace, cross his river, their fence, and his uncle's, and approach the house; he would hear, "Who is out there?" to which he would answer immediately so as not to have an accident and be hit by a blow because of some confusion.

—It's me, uncle, Amando?

Everything was silent, and then suddenly, "What do you want at this hour?"

—What do you want at this hour?

—My father sent me to get a cigarette.

The light in the entrance was lit with a candle flame, and he gave him the cigar along with a quarter from his horse's bridle.

Without crying because he had learned that if he cried, they would give him another one so that he would learn that men hold on and don't cry.

He was a night owl; he learned that the silence of the night made him more active, and during the day, he would take a nap to replenish his eight hours of rest. Whether they were together or in a row, they were never missing from his rest routine.

At the end of the day, when it was almost dawn, he heard in the distance some roosters crowing to announce the dawn. The people seeing what he had done gave him what they could, so he took all the coins to his mother, who cried when she saw him so small and already working; it made her sad.

She prepared lunch and got the family up for breakfast. Time went by, and with it, more children, completing five more in total. Her two older brothers came from time to time to greet their mother without giving them much help; they were already making their own lives.

He used to undertake jobs as a loader's assistant, delivery man, and mechanic, all of them temporary. The conditions of the place were not enough to satisfy so many needs. To his good fortune, he got a job in a nearby quarry, where he started from the bottom and liked sculpting the quarry; he learned very quickly and became an assistant to the master, so they offered him a permanent job. They would do work in Querétaro, four or five hours from the capital. He liked the idea. They continued in his life until one day, when he returned home and found his father waiting for him, he told him:

—Your mother already told me from work that you would travel, and the answer is: No! You don't move from here, and I don't give you my permission.

He retired to his bed to sleep. He thought he was drunk and that he would get over it the next day. The next day, he left early for work, and when he arrived, he saw that his father was leaving.

He felt a knot in his stomach—a bad feeling. He recognized that, with his father's actions, nothing good would be behind him. He settled in as usual, and the manager told him to go by his payment and that they could not keep him there or they would get into trouble with Don Margaro. So he did, and, full of anger and frustration, he took one of the two trucks that would take him home, which, because of the time of day, was not so crowded, so the driver, trusting him and seeing his face, made small talk. There he unloaded his pain and frustration, stressing that he was his father and that it was his fault for not obeying.

The driver, named Pedro, told him that there was no problem and that he could go with him as a collector on the bus; automatically, his face changed, and he paid attention to the indications of the terminal and the bus number. He returned home happy, and without saying a word, he hugged his mother. He never trusted her again. He loved her; however, he would not go through this experience again because of his father.

He became a more reserved person, and he only kept his unconditional friendship with his older sister, Adelina, with whom they were always thick as thieves.

The next day he went out, walking as far as he could to the indicated place, arriving still in the dark. The watchman asked him, "What are you doing here?", He explained the reason and that Pedro had hired him, so he was coming to prepare the truck. The watchman let him pass, changed his clothes, put on his old clothes, and got ready to wash the bus. Then he washed and put on his work clothes again. When Pedro arrived, he liked the actions of washing the bus and arriving early. That was the beginning of their friendship because Amando, a loyal and principled person, always maintained his gratitude for that action.

Over the years, he learned how to win over the people of that place, always trying to keep the area clean. He helped others with the mechanics and the cleaning of the units and learned everything quickly, which facilitated his tasks. He learned to drive, and everyone there appreciated him and gave him some teaching that made him improve. The manager of the bus line introduced him to the owner, and he immediately liked him; he already knew about him, so he wanted to meet him. With their friendship, he asked him for a chance to drive a bus, to which he replied:

—As soon as you bring me your license, I will give you the bus; I will buy a new one for you.

As soon as he was old enough, he got his license, and they gave him a new bus for himself but not for the city. He began to make short trips to the cities near the capital and from there to other states until they sold the line to another person, who gave him one condition: he had to hire "Don Amando." He already had that gift that implies respect for others.

In doing so, Don Amando brought Pedro with him. He said gratitude should never be left aside; a person who is not grateful tends not to be honest because he does not recognize those who lend him a hand.

He was able to help his family more in his own way, and with his absences, he knew how to be economically present, making his sisters finish their short careers at the time, with which he was satisfied with his effort.

His fame preceded him. His height, grace, presence, and good education opened the doors to many opportunities, which would lead him to have a very particular personality, allowing him to talk to all kinds of people and earn their respect. That is how those who knew him referred to him as "Don Amando," a gift given by the respect one earned in those times. The gift was important because it made it clear that this person was respected, indicating his authority, trust, loyalty, honesty, and word.

This situation marked him as an obligated man, never like his father, who was hard-working and well-managed, which allowed him all his life savings. A gesture that would reach one of his older brothers, Cheto, who cunningly managed to persuade him, told him that they would start a business and that, as brothers, they would know how to make it prosper, starting with a bus and then another, and so on until they created their own bus line. At first, he lacked confidence, but this was his older brother; they were blood and flesh of the same parents, and as different as they were, so he did not hesitate and fell under the nets of the words that made him believe that he should trust fully, without papers, for that the word was enough.

Surrendering his savings and trust, he continued his work until the time they had agreed upon was given. There was nothing. There was nothing. He lost everything; there was a family conflict, and there were sides that supported or criticized him for having trusted him without documents to prove the deal. He left his word in doubt against his brother, who said that it was his, that he had bought it with sacrifices, and that now Amando saw an advantage in it.

This made him extremely distrustful. He already had the first blow nailed in his chest, breaking not only the trust but also the illusions he had had with this business.

He continued his life, becoming more reserved. He got married for the first time to an older woman. They had six daughters, all women, and that weighed heavily on his manhood. Although he did not say anything, it was like a dagger that stuck in him and that he avoided commenting on. He separates, and over the years, he has an affair, through which he has one more daughter. I think he once thought about how life gave him these tests.

Suddenly, his older brother appears, apologizing and imploring for his forgiveness, making him believe that he was wrong, that he acted badly, and that he was paying for it. He believed in his repentance, wept, and knelt before him. Only a man, when he cries, is sincere. They are not given to crying; that is for old women. They usually cry for everything, but for no reason, she thought and knelt before him; this spoke of true repentance.

He gave her a hug and wiped the slate clean; the past is forgotten. Not a week went by when he begged for her help again; he told her:

—Let me repay you for the previous favor! Trust me: I will more than happily pay you back your money. Now we will make a line of cargo transportation; let's make a company together.

Distrustful, but at the same time wanting to help, they went together to hitch up a trailer, the first of many, as they both expressed happily. They arrived at the agency. Don Amando gave the down payment, signed the papers, and everything would be paid in a year. The signed letters were left, sealing the operation.

He never stopped sending the payments and continued with his busy work schedule. Now he was the supervisor and route administrator for the line, and he had been in charge of bringing Kenwood trailers for his new employer, who was creating transportation and moving lines. What a coincidence, he thought, that they would be in competition.

At the end of the year, he went to the agency to retrieve the invoice once the payments were settled. What a surprise he got when he discovered that his brother had already picked it up! He felt a pain in the pit of his stomach; something was wrong. He argued with the manager and threatened to sue. Sole was told that he came on the orders of his brother to pick up the bill. Being brothers, they did not give it much importance. At that time, it was not customary to distrust in that way, so they agreed.

She tried to look for him, but he was hiding; she couldn't find him no matter how many messages she had left. She thought everyone was covering for this rat. There is no one honest to make him understand that what he did was a robbery. She had to leave on a trip, so she stayed until dawn, saw him arrive at her house, prevented him from passing, and asked him for an explanation.

—Explanation? Of what or why?

Already, with those words, he knew that the cynic was coming out. He knew this would not end well, both with a gun at the belt. At that moment, the wife came out. She begged for the life of her husband, who, upon seeing her condition of bravery and fear of anything, lowered his arrogance three notches. Don Amando would not let his face be seen again, and this rat did not deserve to be alive, she thought. He couldn't face the pleas of his wife, who was shouting at his daughters to come out and help their father, little girls who didn't understand what was going on. Angrily, he told her to continue behind his wife's skirts, that someday they would settle the score and retire.

On one occasion, he worked as a police commander and was a bodyguard for his boss, only in different areas, so he was allowed to be armed. He even had several permits to carry a gun, so he said that if you carry a gun, it is to use it, not as an ornament.

On one occasion, as the years went by, a daughter asked him:

—Have you killed someone, dad?

To which he answered very seriously, with a frown, "'Be thankful that no one has killed your father."

With this, he said everything, and it is better not to find out what you don't want to know.

His life passed this way, leaving him closed to being open again with his family. With everyone around him, they broke his heart again, and there was no turning back. His heart was filled with anger—a hatred that came out of his mouth, not against his brother. This was against him for having fallen twice to the same devil. He took his doses of poison every time this talk came out for some reason and relived it as if it had happened at that very moment. He never got over it; this poisoned his beautiful soul, leaving him blind with anger that never dissipated until his death. He was taking his doses of poison and waiting for them to take effect.

He let this fact pass, but he never recovered. There was no more apology, forgiveness, or plea to make him forgive what his brother did to him. There was never again a relationship between them; there were two or three coincidences where he always very deliberately avoided him.

His travels would no longer be limited to the states. Now that he wanted to flee as far as he could, he accepted trips abroad, to the borders with Belize and Guatemala. Even in the United States, with routes that took him farther and farther, the border brought him many lessons, other cultures, and other types of influences that were never for him. From the south came the spoke of poverty and the principles of culture. From the north, the man spoke of progress, economy, welfare, and what he was always used to.

His boss called and told him he had several tasks for him, including importing trailers and supervising. He felt that life was smiling at him again. He never liked the energy in the neighboring country. He used to say that life was somewhat dissipated and without commitments until, at the border, he would see the woman who would steal his heart forever. The one who could reach his waist with her hands was short in height; he was almost two meters; he did not care; she was much smaller than him; he would not give it much importance; she was an angel, he used to say—very beautiful, educated, different.

He would wait for the next trip to court her. Returning to Mexico City, today CDMX, he looked for a way to schedule another trip to the border, to that place, to see her again, to court her. He did not care about the distance that, without the communication that we usually have nowadays, imposed very large gaps.

Upon his return, he looked for her, asking how to get to Rome in those times. With signs from everyone, he finally found her; both were smitten, or perhaps it was his need to feel that there was someone to care about. Soon after, they decided to live together; they did not want to separate. Both had a history behind them; although she was many years younger, it did not matter, and love arose between them, more in him. Over the years, they married, thus sealing the commitment of the relationship. She was very Americanized; she did not know much about Mexican culture. For her, the machos were the ones in the movies who rode horses, used guns, and fell in love with songs. She did not give much importance to the culture. She came to live in the capital of Mexico without imagining that this machismo would someday break her illusions, dropping her idealism on her love and turning him into a man of mud that, when falling to the ground, broke into many pieces.

She was divorced with a son, whom she left in charge with his aunt and uncle in the United States, with the promise from her beloved that they would soon return for him, just waiting to settle in. She bought a new house for them where they would start their family. The first child, a boy, her son, the one who would preserve the family name and her legacy, was satisfied. He wanted no more; at last, his life would have meant She, motherless, wanted a big family, so she followed this one with four more women and closed with a flourish with another boy, the last one they would have.

They had a very strong relationship. They were opposite poles that attracted each other; their closeness caused sparks. He tried for years to know how to handle the situation of machismo. At the beginning, he said, "My life, you don't need to work; for that, there is your man who can support you; neither can you handle it if you are pregnant; I don't want you to expose yourself, and with so many children, I can't do it. However, her restless spirit gave her no respite. Both were good at selling; they always had business in hand; she, for her part, did not say anything to him, and he, for his part, gave everything to her to keep. Both were very visionary and thrifty.

Because of his travels, he was rarely at home. This worked to perfection because their macho explosions cooled at a distance where both missed each other and forgot everything when they saw each other, showing that their love prevailed.

What hurts machismo is that only they can do it; the others do not count. They end up having the authority to blows or insults by force, or by imposition or fear, and they become prey to their own fears, jealousy, and distrust, aided by alcohol. They take intervals that become more constant until there is no reason or word that makes them react; they stay in their idea, and it is difficult to get them out of there.

It is with blows and threats that they want to achieve everything until, at a certain point, the victims of their mistakes have to learn to live with them, thus eclipsing their identity and their life itself, or simply say, "Enough," and run as far away as possible.

He led her to this. She thought that his love would not let her give up and that everything good he gave her, in the end, would come out right. Only briefly, the scales tipped a little towards her, and she didn't think twice. She escaped his death trap and was free.

He cursed her in every possible way and spent sleepless nights with the light off, illuminated by the lit cigarette that would not go out, a sign of thoughts that constantly tormented him. He did not understand what had happened. That's how macho men were—men, those who begged, "Hurt me, hit me, kill me, but don't leave me!"

So many blows, so many humiliations, so many deceptions, and so much pain ended up ending their relationship. At every moment of his days, he showed courage towards her until, being very young, she, much younger than him, stopped living and went to eternal sleep. When he found out, he could not contain himself. Tears ran down his eyes. He prayed for her all the time and explained to God that he wanted her alive, even if she was with someone else far away from him. That's what he said were lies! Words of a hurt man who only spoke for the sake of speaking; he wanted to turn back time, but we will never know for what: maybe forgiveness that he never dared express or a kiss that was left hanging in the air, claiming its moment. He simply could not resist it, and sometimes he said he deserved to die, not her.

Life is like that. That's why in life, let's give what we owe so as not to be left with weights that harm and scourge us, and much less let's ask for what we don't really want.

His children one day brought her ashes to him at his request; he made an altar for them; he embraced the urn, kissed her, called her, and talked to her. You could feel his pain —the one that could never overcome his machismo, that macho that does not give his arm to twist, the one that does not know how to beg or ask for forgiveness.

An American who knew him could perceive him as he was, as a worthy representative of the males, and said that he only lacked the horse, to which he replied that now they were called carts.

The one who said the woman was like the shotgun, loaded and behind the door,

To which the gringo said: "Mr. Amando, you are the last macho man of this country. Your genius and figure will never leave you, and I am proud to know you. It is a satisfaction to be your friend; what I regret is that you have never allowed yourself to keep a woman by your side".

—Those women are no longer left, my friend, — he replied. They are now modernized; they can't stand so much. Women from before—women like my mom, who died on the line quietly, without saying a word, accepting everything my father did to her— She was a saint.

In the end, his greatest terror came true; he did not want to die alone, but he did not allow his children to show him their love. Already having grandchildren and great-grandchildren, he gave himself to them in dribs and drabs. He believed they should approach him; he was the father, grandfather, and great-grandfather. It was his duty.

Something that we children do not usually understand is how to give something that we have not been taught. And if you approach, there are only reproaches and offenses. Those memories we usually make as children—by nature, we usually make normal mistakes—that he could not understand stole his childhood. He had to learn to be a man; he had no choice. His responsibilities were acquired by force of his father's indifference—that man who, at the end of his days, also had to help; he was his father, and his mother taught him so. Her father is not good, bad, crooked, or right, and he is not to be judged. That's what God is for; he is the only one who can.

Suddenly, one of his daughters heard him; she saw him in a bad way. She visited him with his family—the children, the grandchildren, the son-in-law—and they gave him an unforgettable visit. They asked him, they begged him to go with them, but he disagreed. He said that that was his home and that he would not move from there. Something was not right: something in her look; her fighting spirit was being lost; maybe it was her age; she was already old; the years are not forgiving.

She returned the following week. He was in his sarong, sitting in a chair, very Pedro Paramo-like, sunburned, and without the strength to get up, his skin stiffened by the weather. "What happened, Daddy?" he asked tearfully, to which he replied that he had had an unpleasantness with one of his sisters, that she had a lawyer son, and they wanted him to sign some documents:

—They are vultures who sense my death and want a piece of what is mine. Let them work, not a lot of money, not a lot of wealth? And always living by the day, dreaming other people's dreams. I didn't sign anything; they're crazy. What lawyer or anything! If it were good enough for them, they wouldn't come for what I have; I'm not so stupid, and I can still defend myself, and if they don't understand by hook or by crook, then by crook.

—He's just like his brother, such thieves as La Chetita and Chetito. They are a bunch of thieves, which is advantageous.

—What if I take care of you, *manito*?

—"What little hand, or what the hell?"

He was right, and his character too; only his strength was disappearing. He was lucid and firm in his decisions and thoughts.

That scene gave me sadness. That man of strong character was giving in to the nature that had already claimed his body; this one, who lived and enjoyed life in his own way, had to continue.

In the end, love wins in a situation like this. Three sisters organized themselves; one even thought of opening a nursing home. It was better than seeing him alone. She did not want to travel and could not leave her goods, which she swore she would take with her to the afterlife. In the end, a single sister stayed with him, and another who had not spoken to him for more than twenty years took care of his food for the next few weeks.

Six weeks after the dream or premonition, Don Amando died and was buried in a simple tomb, a man who had survived everything. He left a life full of teachings, and his memory is well remembered by many. He did good things in his own way, and with that understanding, they were good for him. So how will someone judge who, in his mind, does not realize that something is wrong? Although he used to say that he who ignorantly sins ignorantly condemns himself, I don't believe it; God knows the intention of our hearts. He here paid for everything he did and what he didn't do as well. As a macho man, he knew how to resist every eventuality, overcoming everyone and never stealing from a brother or abusing his trust.

Macho, a party animal, womanizer, gambler, hard worker, and honest man, stopped living to continue riding on a cloud, so he, alone, knew what life was in his own way.

—I am here, by the door, watching the dawn and watching when you were leaving, following the path of the sky. Where the sky began to open in lights, moving away, more and more faded among the earth's shadows.

CHAPTER VI
THE DOG OF THE COLONY

—One lawyer with his briefcase can steal more than a hundred men with guns.

The worst dog is usually better than the worst person; not so the dog of the colony, that one that, at a kicking point, was taught to bite even those of his own family.

It is good to recognize that the dog is considered man's best friend, the one that is usually the faithful squire and gives so much joy to their owners. Good pets are faithful and unconditional beings, those who would give their lives to save ours.

But today, we will not talk about these, but about that one that never felt satisfied with what he was given, that one that, for wrong reasons, always looked for his benefits. This kind of rabid animal that does not think and usually bites anyone who approaches it is usually called the dog of the colony, and it goes around scaring and biting anyone who crosses its path. His own interests blind him; he has lost empathy for others, not even for the trials life imposes on him. It usually makes him show a little kindness or consideration, focused on what his ends mark him.

It is the story of a lawyer who goes through life trying to be the best lawyer, who does not stop to think about professional ethics and instead does whatever it takes to achieve his goals, who does not care about forging signatures, bribing public ministries, giving bribes, as long as he achieves his goals, who dreams of maintaining a life of luxury that only appears, who owes what he has and does not have what he owes—a person who has not seen

Families usually have dreams among us; we all try to get ahead in the same way, but as we grow up, we take separate paths due to circumstances; there is always a black sheep, sorry, a dog of the colony that is detached from the values, principles, morals, and ethics that should be had and wanders his way. Sometimes I believe that it is his mother, blinded in her love, believing that goods give level among a society to which they do not belong and to which they dream to belong, that making him believe that he is doing the right thing clouds his sight and allows him to give bites justifying his actions, even if they are of his own family.

One day, a very special case came up where an uncle of his had died, and he had tried to get him to give him the authority to administer his estate, promising him that he would do the right thing and respect his last will. His uncle disagreed; it was not his will. He went several times, accompanied even by his mother, and they never got a single signature from him.

He died, and then, in the following events, as it usually happens in cases where there is no will, with the family divided, he saw the weakness of the relationships between them and approached the most vulnerable people, who, for lack of preparation, study, or sensitivity to the relationship of siblings, fell into his nets, without understanding the maneuver that would be carried out, because somehow, they assumed that he would benefit them regardless of the damage.

They created a distortion of reality, an alternative that would make them feel more at peace with themselves, justifying their actions to achieve their purposes. He told them things, used flattering words, and thus took them away from others to manage them in his own way. With wrong beliefs contrary to what is healthy, there enters the adage, "Divide and conquer. That is how he did it. He spoke to them, so they fell into his clutches without realizing they were acting wrongly. In the end, the dog bites through his mouth, and someone comes along to burn his nose so that he learns that everything has limits.

Nobody had ever been in this situation until, due to the insecurity in the country, a brother, the eldest, fell into misfortune, having nowhere to live; he had the bad luck to be extorted and threatened, and they killed one of his workers; he had to flee overnight; he had to leave his company, his patrimony, to flee from the threat. He wandered from here to there, rolling around, until he realized that the house his father used to live in was abandoned, so it was easy for him to go and live there. When the sisters found out, they called their cousin, the neighborhood dog, who would try to bite and make the intruder bleed until he understood that this was not his territory. The lawyer wanted him out without considering his relative, so he sued. They went to the legal instances, both parties hired lawyers, and the sides were formed: in one, three brothers, two of another, and another that was still undecided. Seeing the situation, two more brothers joined him; they had as much right as all those who considered themselves the owner's sons.

He could not get it out; the legal instances did not allow it; some lawyers know the law and play fair, so, not being able to do it through legal channels, the lawyer's mother, the aunt, wanted to talk to them. She said nonsense things, like your father told me that the assets were for them, to which the answer was a resounding no; the three were advised, one woman and two men. During the trial, a lawyer close to the family was hired. She discovered a lot of irregularities in the trial, where signatures were forged, there was an attempt to sell the assets without an official resolution or papers, addresses were altered, and a thousand other things that only a person without principles or morals would do when dealing with the family.

The mother continued with the communication and expressed that, if it were up to her, the brother could live on the street, a situation that made it clear what kind of people they were. However, not all of them, because the father and the brothers do not usually agree with these acts; in fact, this appellative towards him came out among them.

They said that he was so bad at what he did that he always won the trials this way, that he did not try his heart out for them, that they had gone through situations in which they had been affected, and that he used to tell them: "This is work, it is not family". So they nicknamed him the dog of the neighborhood.

They then reinforced the legal strategy. The trial went on for two years. Unfortunately, the reason for this trial became meaningless when the older brother, who was very young, suffered an accident and lost his life a few months after the accident. His well-being, being the only reason for this trial to have a place to live, vanished with his departure.

The illusion of everything being him; the strategies to obtain something were for him; the other two brothers stopped insisting on this, understanding that things are not won this way. His father, before he died, said: "I am not going to leave anything to anyone; I prefer that they kill themselves for it."

Without a real desire regarding the thing in dispute, the actions are dissolved, making clear what a person close to both said: "If your sisters hired him, it is because they have the same way of seeing things; this negative energy will only bring them salt and water." "Leave things to time; he is already starting to pay for his mistakes."

We cannot go through life being that dog who wants to bite everyone, that bully who intimidates everyone with his actions, who wears a suit, and who smells rich to cover the smell of rottenness inside; that's life; we are blinded by goods that end up meaningless and without reason. More great treasures have been forgotten by civilizations, sunk in the depths of the seas, kingdoms exchanged for a horse, and families are now fighting for something so minimal that it has even further divided families.

The approaches we give to things are the prices we pay, so we must put a price on things, not on people, and stop seeing those who sell us mirrors with wonderful conditions; we must pay the price we will end up paying.

In the end, not only does death usually bring pain to those who remain here, but the consequences of our actions end up catching up with us and making us prey to our own mistakes—a poison that ends up killing us little by little and in life.

I am glad to know that there are usually people who build their goods, unlike others who want to appropriate them, and on that they have based their lives. In the end, it is not the one who has more goods who is happier, but the one who can go to rest every night with a clear conscience.

But the question that should come to our minds is:

How many of us have been, are, or will be the dogs of the colony?

Have we ever stopped to think that the end will never justify the means, and if so, how happy will we be? Will we really enjoy being this way, or will we hire someone to give us what we think we deserve at the cost of many other things? Will we be able to live in peace and enjoy it to the fullest? If so, it will be that we lack conscience, which usually reminds us of what is right, does not leave us alone when we do not do things right, and usually torments us with our mistakes. Will we be able to keep it silent? Maybe, but it will always, sooner or later, rumble in our minds, charging every affront of our bad actions and showing us the prices we pay for them. Ignore it?

Learning to hire a professional or be a professional must be with an ideology like ours, so we will not give wrong ideas that confuse our reality and those of others.

Thinking before making a decision to do the right thing, preventing before regretting, doing what goes according to universal values, opening our eyes wide to capture the energies that go according to an elevated way of life with good purposes, and teaching our children, students, and people around us—not only with words but also with actions—that everything works better and gives fewer problems if it is done in the best way Actions and preventions will prevent the emergence of more dogs in the colony, leading us to more decadence than what already abounds today. In the end, they will also participate in the consequences that we will receive, so it is our duty to pay attention to this and to do the right thing in a formal and legal way so that everything is well established, without leaving problems or situations that break family relationships, and to avoid conflicts that sweep, with vested interests, in bad ways that allow others to abuse the vulnerability of the mourners.

Let us change the energies of our planet, let us seek to counteract that which is doing so much harm and attracting things that scare us or make us afraid or ashamed, and let us be human beings that have love, empathy, kindness, service, helping, progressing in the right way, that elevate us to that state of satisfaction, so that we can achieve harmony and control of our lives with our eyes wide open to any wrong signal.

Let us strive to educate with values and principles, in union and harmony, creating bonds that teach, that educate, and that transcend in others with all the good we can. Let us teach our children to be good brothers, good people, good parents, good professionals, good bosses, and good employees, and that they find satisfaction in it, and when they make mistakes that they do not fail to be aware of the amendment and forgiveness, making them see that the opposite of what is right will never be a good way.

—Lawyers are men we hire to protect us from other lawyers.

—I sometimes criticize lawyers, but I reconsider my remarks when I need the services of one.

—Lawyers are the only people not punished for ignorance of the law.

CHAPTER VII
THE BAGS OF POOP

Only when the mind is free of ideas and beliefs can it act correctly.

Krishnamurti

Freedom comes when we remove all the burdens we carry, those weights that we have accumulated during our lives, sometimes dead weights that have no function, yet we carry them with us.

The shadows are chasing us because we create and give power to them without realizing that, in return, we lose who we really are.

We think we know who we are! It is not true; we are running away from everything. Without realizing all that we have created, we imagine great walls, precipices, mountains, mighty rivers, and wild beasts that keep us under control, and we strive to do so. We hide all that we believe about ourselves, our true personality, with its desires and tastes, in such a way that it goes unnoticed between what we appear and what we hide, only giving a glimpse from time to time of our repressions. These shadows usually appear in our defeats, our difficult trials, and the unfinished chapters that we have not accepted.

Hiding everything behind appearances, without allowing ourselves the freedom that will allow us to fly and cross other horizons, those acts of kindness towards ourselves where we allow ourselves to believe, feeling the joy that this implies What prevents us from doing so? Our dark shadows magnify their power before us and dwarf us through time, stopping us from fighting and believing that we can do it all.

We tend to see that everything harasses and invades us with terrible feelings that limit our freedom and way of seeing things. We grow up believing that this is so; can we never overcome these burdens? We begin to conform, allowing the light to become a thick fog that makes us stumble in its gloom, failing so many times without seeing the light again, the one that invited us to continue until we could touch it and feel its peace.

We feel so small! We make our greatness begin to suffocate with our mind; its voices do not allow us to have quiet times to think on our own.

What are we carrying?

Everything we have allowed ourselves. That which we believe so well that it becomes part of our beliefs.

Many years ago, I used to take swimming lessons. I entered the splash pad with my brothers and sisters, one of the oldest, along with other children in the same class. As the months went by, no matter how hard I tried, I could tell that I was not progressing. I didn't quite understand what was going on, but something inside me accepted that reality. I knew I was doing certain tricks because I didn't have much confidence in the water, and the class teacher let everyone advance but me; I stayed in a new group without making progress. I guess I didn't pay attention to the indications, or I didn't do it correctly, or the instructor didn't take me seriously; any situation didn't benefit me! As time went on and I was growing up, there was a moment when I accepted my defeat and gave up on the classes. I stopped going, but something inside me gave me anger for not having succeeded and for the fact that everyone else could have more fun when interacting with somebody of water, to which I had to be just an observer of this fact without being able to participate.

Over the years, I had the opportunity to learn many things, except how to swim, so I tried to avoid this fact so that it would not hurt me. Until I realized that this barrier would not only affect me but could also affect my children, I thought about it repeatedly and could not bring myself to ask them for something that "I had not achieved". Was it wanting our children to live our dreams? That's not how it should work until I lived the experience of being a mother.

They usually come to the rescue; they make us expel our fears, do incredible things, and achieve everything we set out to do. It is they or other beings that fill us with energies that make us want to walk the second mile, fly as high as possible, cross seas in storms, and eat the world with our fists; some may call it love; for others, it will be the engine, and the purpose will always be the same: to improve ourselves.

With the first, I could understand that this love crossed the lines of time and the universe and that distances do not matter; he removed the blindfold from my eyes and made me see that his birth had a purpose that filled my life and that of his brothers with benefits, and he made me believe in the fragility and the power that lie in it.

With the second, I felt that joy in my heart to give protection, to feel her warmth and that new smell that emanates milk and honey, to have the most sublime feelings with her little body in my hands; that power gives: courage, emotion, motivation, and it made me grow, mature, and be better. It generated a commitment that, to this day, I maintain with them, but with her, it was created. That fragility that fills them with strength comes with the magic of watching them grow, accepting them, and helping them to be themselves, the ones who set their own pace; what if we like it or not? It is our problem since they come to live their own lives, not ours.

The third of the great challenges that confine us in worlds of confusion are those where, despite being the same, they do not avoid fitting in. Could it be the beauty of our authenticity? It lies there; it is to be unique and special, and I understood it better with him, and he made me respect what they are with more awareness. They are our sons and daughters; they do not belong to us; we are guardians responsible for their integrity, protection, and education.

Ah! But the last one was the one that moved my world; at this moment, I found myself. As many say, I was born again; I had a new opportunity, and I understood that I was not living but just coexisting in a world full of beings like me, full of everything but life, like ghosts that wander here and there and back and forth without realizing what this means. We stop feeling; we stop being aware that life will be a fleeting moment that fades away so fast, but so fast that it disappears when we want to start living, and it's too late; time and opportunities are over with it.

That's when we become foolish people, filling bags with nothing but slowing ourselves down.

When I understood this situation, I felt extremely sad. I saw my failures, and I could realize that I had learned from my mistakes and how not to do things. I learned that tests hurt me and that I usually suffer for something I cannot control, leaving me to enjoy what I do have, what I can do, and what I should do. My fears, those shadows that no matter how hard I have run, are part of my own nature, and I am the only person who has allowed them to grow, before because I could not control them and now because I do not want to; however, I can control their power until they disappear.

At this moment when the lives of both were in danger, that significant and cruel destiny that usually makes us understand by hook or by crook our mistakes and demands their payment made us prisoners. Leaving aside the pretexts, those "buts" cease to have importance, and they submerge us in that valley of more shadows. We have no choice but to let us faint or rebel, to rise again, better, stronger, begging God, expressing to the universe, to the superior energy that forgives us! We are good if we can, if we must, that it is now or never our change, and that we will do better.

It was when I saw my orphaned mother tell her stories filled with so much pain that I did not want my children to live with them. I felt that feeling running through my soul, and I wanted to push it away. I asked, I begged, I pleaded until I stopped feeling; everything calmed down, it became a dream, and when I woke up, I heard my father's voice calling me in the distance; he was shouting my name in desperation. I woke up, I saw myself alive, and I wanted to scream! I could not; my mouth did not express any words; at that moment, my strength returned little by little to my body; I sent him a message giving him tranquility; I had to be well for my baby, for my daughters, for my son, for me...

For the second time, I was leaving a hospital with nothing to carry but with the hope of returning for her in two weeks. The days were passing slowly, and in dribs and drabs was the opportunity to be with her; however, she was alive, unlike the first one that failed to overcome the challenge that she had to face, leaving that eternal hole that I hope someday to fill with her, at some point in the beyond of this physical world. Two weeks in which I was able to realize that I wanted to live, that I would be willing to make the necessary changes so that they did not carry what did not correspond to them, and to teach them by example that one can always do it when one is willing to do it. I don't know if I have done a good job, but I have done my best, and best of all, they will never let me give up, much less let it defeat me.

Two weeks in which I was able to make plans, redirect my life, and understand who I was and how special I should be to me and let others know it. Only this way would I make my children not repeat those stories that we end up believing and carrying as truths that hinder every step we take, making the falls more and more painful, making us believe that there is no road that leads us to another place, that we must conform to what we are told and be crude copies of others.

I rebelled, understanding came fully into my being, I embraced my faith and stopped feeling less, believing that I could not, and receiving my little girl in my arms was the beginning of conscious changes in me. I stopped living in the past, and I stopped complaining about everything I had lived; now, I count it as one of the experiences that made me know how I should not do things, and I investigate how I should do it. I learn from the best; I look for this knowledge to come from those who have something good for me. Some ways of living, doing, being, learning, or creating—even though fears continue to corner me from time to time—I usually throw myself into finding out if I can do it better.

After we were both able to get out of this critical situation, the first thing I did was learn to swim. In two weeks, I achieved what I could not achieve in years. In the two weeks in which I hired the best course with the best teacher and achieved it, it was not expensive at all; in fact, it was in a community center in the city, but the class gave me what I was looking for, the teacher understood my challenge, he shared the commitment, and we both managed to get this knowledge right. There was a connection to what I was determined to learn. Afterward, I was able to teach my daughters and my son, all in their own way and in their own time, in the same way that I was taught. When the student is ready, the teacher appears! I was ready, and my children were ready. So determined to put my learning into practice, I went to the beach with my older brother, and he took me to a place where, on a cliff, I jumped into the open sea. He was there with me when, being in that place, we started to talk, and suddenly he says to me, "I thought you didn't know how to do it.

I thought you did not know how to swim.

I answered:

I didn't know! I just learned how to...

He didn't let me finish; he panicked, and without letting me finish, he demanded that I get out, to which I replied, "If I haven't learned correctly, I'm not going to swim."

If I have not learned correctly, you are here to save me, and if not? I will have to pay the price for not having learned correctly, and I will have the consequences of the risks that this implies, under my own responsibility and without letting others take the blame for it. Although in the beginning I felt some fear, I usually realize that the more I think about it, the more doubts I have, and then I enter that state of nervousness or paralysis and stop acting.

Then I think: "What does not move is wasted; what is wasted, and rots is useless; and if it is useless, it is discarded, thrown away." So, I must be in constant movement.

It was not the same with my children; with them, I was more careful; I helped them have confidence, enjoy the moment, develop their skills, and achieve this goal that meant so much to me. The best thing about it is that they learned so fast that we were in perfect sync, in the same tune, at the same level, at the right time, in the right way, and it just flowed. There were no barriers or false information that changed how they saw this moment. There was no cheating. I enjoyed this so much that I learned that this is how it would be for everything in their lives.

I used to get on the highest trampoline or the highest waterfall and just jump, trying to perform my jump in the best way, without fear...

I've occasionally fallen perfectly, other times not so much, and occasionally experienced scares that make me grateful that I always control the risks and that they do not have serious consequences because of my imprudence. I jump, which is my freedom, without weights or listening beyond my voice. Grateful for that will that we all have and that letting it out creates powerful people.

Can it be that there are no others to motivate us, can it be that we feel alone, that the shadows want to leave us in their hands in terror of doing something that matters to us, learning that "we" are the most important beings to us, and "I" am without my ego the person who counts the most in our own lives?

When taking a flight somewhere, the first thing we are told goes something like this:

If cabin pressure is lost, the oxygen masks will come off automatically.

First, put them on yourself, and then help others around you, including people who are more sensitive to the situation, such as children, the elderly, or sick people.

If you are a healthy, strong person who can do this job, do it and help others.

If you (I) are not, then you are a person who needs help, so expect assistance from someone who already has an oxygen mask on.

A simple example of the reality we have—seeing the crystal-clear water waiting for us and being afraid—prevents us from learning to lose the fear and just lets us live consciously, with controlled risks prevailing for my safety and the safety of others, first and foremost.

To understand in the right way that I am the most important person. To teach, we must learn to stop imposing ourselves and try to impose on others those things so villainous that lead us through life carrying our things in the wrong way, for carrying everything that others put on us without being able to say No!

That power teaches us to stop being stressed or depressed by something that is not in us. Yesterday something happened that made me recognize that I need to stop learning from my mistakes and look for professionals with the right knowledge who make me feel like I can do it with the right tools.

Imagine that we want to cut down a huge tree with a dull kitchen knife.

We are a seed of science, with the perfect technology, endowed with an infinite database and the option to store everything that comes to us; now, we must learn to select the right way to store in priority what will make us better.

We are perfect, perfectible in what we still need to improve, and unique among the millions of human beings that have inhabited, inhabit, and will inhabit this world, so we are as special as our uniqueness. We must not forget that we are born this way, being able to improve, never letting us lose our life before we die physically, enjoying and living every moment in the here and now, leaving the attachments that hurt us, and respecting others without judging them, much less falling into gossip or things that hurt us or hurt others.

Letting go of being afraid of the old man in the sack, the monster under the bed, the bogeyman, the boogeyman, the future, the past, the present, to do it or not to do it, to what they say, and I do not care, and if I care, I will look for a table of values to see the weight that this has on me.

So we are the ones who can overcome everything and let those little bags that we usually carry with us not make us carry more than we should.

When we were little, my mother used to do the cleaning, looking to control her children in bed so we wouldn't get into mischief. I don't remember how it happened; I only know that we couldn't get out because the monster under the bed would grab us by the feet! I don't know how this started, but in the end, there were six of us in bed, and she was in a hurry, as usual. We followed the same ritual: if someone wanted to get off, we all tried to hold him down so that he would not be "exposed" to being pulled off his feet. This is how these moments passed when control through fear kept us calm.

As time went by, no one was on top of the bed; we were now helping with the housework. As soon as the night came, no one used to turn off the light in a calm way; we all used to run and jump without going near the base of the bed; fear persisted in its own way in each one of us. As my mother realized this, she started her own way of working with each one of us to overcome this fear. She used to come in at night and have us peek under the bed with a flashlight so we could see that there was nothing there. I know she worked hard to get us to overcome this fear. It wasn't so easy anymore. One day he came to my room and laid down next to me. We began to talk, and from one moment to the next, we were under the bed.

He told me stories, and he made me see this part of the bed so much that it became my favorite place. There, I disappeared. It was so quiet and cool in hot weather, or when it was cold with a blanket, he locked me in a magical world where I could read anything I wanted, and I loved it. Fears were left behind like that place where the space started to get too small that I forgot how good it felt to be there. Fears faded with the passage of time, and just as I overcame this one, I managed to learn to swim and thousands of other things that have helped me to see that the burdens we sometimes carry are often manipulations to gain access to our control, that for whatever reasons they tend to make us prisoners of something that may limit us from growing and moving forward to a fuller being that lives its own exploits, and the worst thing is that we repeat them in others. I do not know if, as revenge or as a strange game that has become part of our lives, those uses and customs, far from forming something good, do as much damage as they can.

RAE definition for "bag": an imbecile person or sack of some kind of material used to carry something.

Two descriptions will go perfectly with those who do not understand that traveling light and lending ourselves to carry or give to others means that, without value, we give so much importance.

The bags are objects that serve us to carry weights without costing us so much effort, or they are people who are fools or lack intelligence. Either definition can serve us because, at the end of the day, we tend to carry other people's things with us, feeling bad for others and making us foolish and insensitive.

It may sound unreal, but it is true. This is the reality that many people live, that many of us live, and the more we try to escape, the more we get entangled in their nets, always ready to make mistakes. In order to get rid of them, gossip, confessions, secrets, and confidences have been invented, and now there are even specialists who can help with them.

We love to communicate everything; we are beings that like to relate through vocal expression; we tend to give it too much importance, so much that we revolve around it; we tend to talk more than we should, paying little attention to understanding what we hear. Interaction generally becomes a channel, always one-way, capturing what, on many occasions, conversations become gossip that, far from bringing something good, usually causes unfortunate situations where "someone" usually gets hurt—hoping not to be us.

To this, we can add that there are certain types of people who see it as a sport; they tend to do bad things, make mistakes, and look for someone to confide in, someone who can keep the secret. If they do not find a professional, they tend to take their "friends," whether they are family members or not, and often tell them about the "bad" things they have done or have learned that "others" have done.

Leaving a brief space for this to become known, affecting their life or that of others by some indiscretion that becomes "gossip," which, when passed from mouth to mouth, whether true or not, carries both poison and bad intentions with faces of innocence.

Gossip, whether true or false, usually causes damage; it is the intention with which it seeks to hurt, not the comment itself as a way of saying, "What do you think...? Look at that... It seeks to draw attention to a fact by giving it too much importance so that others can participate, seeking to judge, attack, and hurt; these conversations will never be well-intentioned, even if we try to disguise that they are well-intentioned.

So, we become fools, carrying, and bringing bags that carry weights that are not ours to carry.

To avoid this type of action, we must open our eyes and see well what type of people we have around us, the trust we "should" have in them, and the weight of the comments.

Our mind always wants to express itself; it must find an answer to everything, so communication becomes a two-edged sword. On the one hand, it makes us feel that we are right, that we give our opinion, that we give our point of view; on the other hand, it makes us feel ashamed, that we are afraid of "what they will say." So if we cannot control our mouths, if this is difficult for us, let's apply these three questions before opening our mouths. We must slow down, make a stop, and think well about what we are going to say or what we are going to hear, the comments, the type of talk, and think clearly about our thoughts so that when they become words, they are heard correctly. We must know if it is formal or informal what we are going to say to know if the people who receive it will have the ability to understand what we want to express or if we are the right ones to listen to what they want to say, so there is an ancient way that was already applied by a great philosopher regarding this for us to apply:

The three filters of this great Greek philosopher, Socrates:

The Truth filter, first test:

"Verify if what you want to express is true."

The filter of goodness, second test:

"What you want to tell me is good."

The Filter of Usefulness, third test:

"Is it USEFUL for me to know?"

Is it true, good, and useful? If it is true that habits are difficult to break, more difficult is to carry in our consciousness unnecessary burdens for not stopping or putting a stop to something that is not true, good, or useful; we should not express it, much less accept it.

Being an unconscious being makes us carry the garbage that others throw in our bags, and we are carrying them, not them; we carry their poop, spoiling, full of flies, and the worst, we are suffering in case someone finds out what would happen to it, without understanding or realizing that the person who does something wrong or makes a mistake comes, discharges his conscience, and continues making his mistakes, thinking that others suffer them. Blocking our energy, altering our vision, and suffering for something that is not ours.

Now we can understand how hard it must be for a pastor, priest, religious psychologist, therapist, counselor, friend, acquaintance, or even a stranger to listen to confessions, keep secrets, offer comfort, and try to help people who are sad. If someone is truly sorry, peace is made between them, and comfort is given even if they don't say a word. However, what if there is no repentance? What if they are just unloading their burdens? What if they are just looking to empty their bags and fill them up again?

We are human beings. There may be events in which we have made mistakes that we are truly sorry for because of some weakness of the flesh, bad decisions, or overconfidence we may have displayed. It is one of the most recurrent ways of learning through trial and error without really realizing if this is true, if it has any value for us to have, or if it has any benefit in our lives.

What people throw at us is not necessarily our choice, but what we do with it is entirely our decision; other people do what they want, but our reaction causes us suffering, and the way we tend to see things and react to them limits our power.

We make excuses for ourselves based on how bad things are and how little we know. We choose these mental states to justify the reasons we give ourselves not to act in a better way without compromising, making lives that are limited to progress limited to the glitter of the world that doesn't let them move forward and see beyond a better world that offers peace and many benefits along with happiness that is no longer a priority.

We avoid the reality we have because of our fears and insecurities, which only make it worse. We are so used to hearing the noises of others that we don't know how to listen to ourselves, giving up our understanding of ourselves, our freedom, and our true selves.

It is then that we tend to understand that we are more concerned about what happens to others; we know more about them than about ourselves.

We're getting more and more wrong, useless, and meaningless information, and it's eating away at everything that should be our top priority. letting us be at its mercy, letting us be possessed in such a way that what happens outside the world is more important than everything else; carrying its weights, its miseries, and meaningless things that keep us from the truth, from reason, and from understanding.

So, we live in a time when we don't really talk to each other, leaving everything to wait for a "like" to say what we don't say. We let appearances today be bubbles of images, allowing all kinds of comments between lovers and haters. We live in the gossipiest world ever, where technology moves fast and people don't talk to each other or show much interest. We see links that connect us to others so easily that we can waste time. When should this give us more power? Access to the power of knowledge. Numbing our emotions and feelings has the effect of leaving everyone empty and confused.

The end can be the beginning if we decide to stop seeing that monster we were taught to see under the bed, or those people who didn't teach us how to swim or let us filter the information we will receive, or if we let ourselves decide right now what I want from my life, here and now, knowing that everything will be as good or bad as we want to see it, that if we think it's wrong or right, we'll be right either way and that I will give the world my best shot.

The end is the beginning of all things, suppressed and hidden. Waiting to be thrown through the rhythm of pain and pleasure.

Krishnamurti

I am indebted to my father (to my parents) for living, but to my (my teachers) master for living well.

Alexander the Great

CHAPTER VIII
HEAVYWEIGHTS

No one has a heavier load than he can carry; he must only see how to carry it; therein lies the science of power.

MBCC

How often do we carry so many things that we think are important? How many times do we blind ourselves by believing that without "it," we cannot live? We carry precious treasures that, over time, begin to lose their value; we begin to remove the blindfold from our eyes, we begin to become aware of where the blindfold disappears, and we begin to see reality with our eyes, ears, and all our senses wide open; we then perceive a reality that we do not like. However, we often do not find a way to cut the circle in which we are trapped.

It begins with the need to feel that state of belonging, which leads us to situations that slowly numb our way of seeing life; in others, we are the ones who blind the vision of others, manipulating them to achieve never-clear objectives. Such a thick fog does not allow us to move in the right direction in our lives; much less are we good company for ourselves and much less for others.

We think that everything that sparkles is gold. We follow fantasies that we think will come true, and we play with them for so long that they become solidified in our minds and start to control our reality. They are like bubbles that pop when we become more aware.

We stop living in the past or the future; although it is not so difficult, it is just hard to do. Committing to breaking habits keeps us captive to certain behaviors that can even kill us in every possible way. To start wanting to escape from these behaviors, we must stop believing that they are of value to us; that which at some point keeps us captive and makes us succumb to it ceases to have the importance it used to; we begin to grow, to understand, to the reason for ourselves, and stop listening to those voices that echo in our mind, keeping us insensitive to our own pain or the pain of those we love most and creating patterns that are repeated in others. Escape? Rather, I think we must first be aware of what it is.

To escape, from whom or from what? Why and for what? To see reality is to bring to light the person who lives trapped inside himself without having his own will, justifying actions so as not to be exposed to give excuses; we stop being people who self-define themselves from their own being and allow limiting beliefs to let others less expert corner us in such a way that we believe what they tell us.

To say we are less experts is to understand that no one can ever know more about us than we do. It's simple; it's just that our ego sometimes gets so inflated that it blinds our understanding to closed conditioning that makes us feel either too much or too little, never in balance. While it is true that extremes are bad, we tend to go from one to the other, avoiding seeing the right way. We are afraid to see who we really are, and we are holding on to that which shines but often lacks value.

Years ago, I understood that people tend to speak about our most obscure actions, facts, or thoughts in order to unload our conscience and allow others to carry our burdens. We were leaving those burdens in the hands of others. Sometimes, for gossip, for confessing something that corrupts us, for therapy—whatever the excuse, pretext, or reality—we must know that there will be a consequence; life is like that; what you send out comes back; the boomerang law; if you are not prepared, it can cause the blow to knock us down in such a way that we do not want to get up again.

Sometimes we are the ones who share something that hurts us or weighs us down, and we want to find that trusted person with whom we can unburden that weight that stuns us, embarrasses us, or fills us with despair. In doing so, most of the time, it turns against us; not only is trust broken, but we also find collateral damage that makes us prey to shame; insecurity is another factor that implodes us inward in such a way that we do not want to get out of there; the damage is done, and we cannot move forward. Thanks to God, the universe, and that powerful energy that invades us and by which we are created, let time do its work.

A blessed time that counts the hours without rest allows every minute and every second to follow its pace without rest, thus allowing all the wounds to heal and those that do not, as a book full of wisdom says: "Cut that which makes you sin, or in my words, cut that which prevents you from growing, continuing, or being complete." - People tend to remain in that pain; it is not that we do not want to continue or do not want to overcome everything that hurts us; it is the terror that takes over us, the fear that paralyzes us, and our mind is filled with things that invade us in such a way that it scares us at the idea of being exposed. On the other hand, if we are the ones who listen to someone's bad deeds, negative situations, or thoughts that torment others, we must also understand the level of responsibility that this implies.

The commitment to trust to tell our sorrows or listen to those of others already carries an implicit risk when we want no one else to know. With the phrase "I want to tell you something, but do not tell anyone". That carries a terrible energy charge; it sounds like gossip, which is not true, does not include us, and has no importance for us, so the value is null. The risk of putting garbage in our minds implies carrying something we do not need. No matter how much we believe that it does not weigh, in the long run, this will become tiring, even worse if we share it, thus failing our honor by expressing something that usually damages not only one person but all those involved when they realize their mistake. No matter how much it may seem that nothing happens, it does happen; there are consequences, and universal laws are never wrong, like universal values that usually go beyond social trends, fashions, or convictions. These usually remain beyond everything and everyone: what is right; what is due in action; actions; and energy that will work in us for good or bad. Where will what is pleasant or unpleasant to us take its toll on our actions?

There is no mistake in the power of creation; the mistake is when we do not take conscience of our actions and we go through life complaining about what happens to us, when absolutely everything that happens to us is a consequence of our actions. If we hear, see, or perceive garbage and warry it with us, we cannot prevent it from spoiling and emitting that smell—energy—that generates the reaction, attracting what we deserve; consciously or unconsciously, this will not prevent it from happening. My father used to say, "He who unconsciously sins, unconsciously condemn himself," and it is true; nothing is truer than this phrase.

The consequences will come claiming with full force; we must be aware that most of them are the cause and effect of our actions, so there is no way to avoid them, although we can seek ways to reduce their impact, change our actions, and change our habits to generate the real change that will prevent us from carrying those weights that destroy us and destroy others.

One day the fair came to town, and all the attractions and stalls were arranged to welcome the public. In that preparation, we find people coming and going everywhere. There are also usually some dogs that are curious about this movement, looking for food or a friendly person. They stay and enjoy the show. One of them saw "the house of mirrors" and decided to enter. With no one at the door, he managed to enter. He begins to see that there are dogs like him, very aggressive; they bother him, and he responds aggressively to the attack they are doing on him, angry and very annoyed; he finally manages to leave, and behind him comes another dog, happy and happy.

He tells him that the experience was not pleasant, to which the other dog replies, "Really, I had an incredible time; everyone was very friendly, and they played with me."

Simple mirrors show us who we really are and how we see the reality we perceive. Simple mirrors reflect who we are; the way our eyes show us is only a matter of focus; we focus on what we have been allowed, what is induced, and where our vision is altered. We see what we have been allowed to see, falling into this game that has led us to carry dead weights that only hinder our walk and make it slow and tiring, leading us to fatigue, a lack of love for life, and losing the real interest that this should have, motivating and generating the energy that leads us to eat the world with our fists.

Years ago, I had several experiences that left me with physical exhaustion and emotional fatigue, where the spiritual role played an important challenge. Many times, we believe that being good people means never saying a few words that prevent others from using us as trash cans to leave their consciences at ease, and we accept to listen and give them support. Unfortunately, they leave and continue to make their mistakes, and we are left with regret.

Certain experiences that marked me in a very significant way were when we sometimes believed that social circles served to create friendships. I think that "can" be possible. However, they usually get out of control and lead us to meaningless experiences, where wasting time is usually the main factor.

The oldest unprofitable occupation is idleness, which is often called the mother of all vices.

That one allows falling into not very honorable acts while justifying the facts to others. For example, one day, I tried to be part of a group at my children's school, where there was a meeting once a week to "socialize". Dropping the kids off at school and having breakfast somewhere or at someone's house was not bad, although, in my mind, I preferred to do other things. To be polite, I agreed. I never saw anyone worried about doing creative things; it was to eat, talk, and finish the race. That time flew by, and we were already late to go anywhere. A fact that did not make me frequent those meetings, so they came to "visit" me. Repeating the cycle, I do not know if I was confident, but I could not say no; I was ashamed of "what will they say," so I agreed with a smile on my face. Little by little, the group was reduced, so I did not stop doing my activities without forgetting the kindness or courtesy of being a host. I was apprehensive about not being in control of my activities, which meant they were the priority in my life. I don't know if people tend to evade their responsibilities or seek an escape from them.

Anyway, as time went by, there were only two people left, and one of them only came to "comment" on what was happening in those meetings -- unimportant things, I think not only for me but also for her -- in her eagerness to bring and bring, she sought to get the conversation going to bring information to those meetings. I have always been a transparent person, so it is not difficult at that point; the problem occurs when we do not know the context or when there is no respect for the individuality of each one. So I found myself in unhealthy situations. We already know the justifications—he doesn't understand me, he doesn't spend time with me, he is distant, he is evil—but they never, ever let the other person know; they face the situation and make a change in their actions. You simply give the conversation a hearing, and that's it. Soon after, the other person finds out and blames me for being the one who spreads the gossip.

First, this act is an escape from the situation. You look for a culprit to get rid of the consequences.

Second, one avoids facing the situation by harming another "momentarily," freeing oneself from the consequences.

Third: causing it to grow like a snowball, which tends to increase as time goes by.

At first, I did not give it the importance it deserved; I thought it was just the original gossip. Even knowing the truth, I preferred to keep quiet. After a while, this person confronted me and shouted. I ignored her. I knew she was a cornered dog trying to avoid the sticks. However, she went about believing that I would not respond to her actions, and so it went for some time, even though I knew the truth from her own words, but I believed it was an act of confession in secret. As this escalated in family circles, I found it necessary to put a stop to it.

I did it so that the type of action she had been taking against me ended. It was a moment in which I confronted her without further consideration; with her own words, I ended this situation. Some people took sides, but she continued with her relationship; after a few years, she separated. I am not happy about it, but it is not our responsibility to carry other people's bags of poop. Let them carry them; sometimes they carry them for so long that they have become accustomed to the smell and no longer perceive it; I can even say that they enjoy it. Their senses have stopped feeling the difference between unpleasant and pleasant, settling for a state of profound insensitivity, so they continue to carry their bags everywhere without understanding the weight that this implies and occasionally throwing part of their weight to others.

This happened to me not once, but many times until I said, "Enough!" I learned to say "no," to receive and open myself to what I wanted to put in my mind. Like this example, many times more than I would like, sometimes I feel that I have become an accomplice to actions with which I disagree. However, paralysis invades me, and I could use more than my principles, values, right thoughts, and those universal laws that are always in force despite the time.

Opening my eyes and letting this feeling overwhelm me again, I raise my voice, I withdraw, I change my actions so that this implies putting a stop, and if it is me, I stop my words, calm my emotions, and start thinking: is it good, truthful, will it do good?, changing the internal sound of my own voice so that I leave that moment and start running away from this that can cause me to harm or hurt others.

To say that I can be the one who carries these bags and wants to water their contents or be the subject of comments or different actions directed towards me, allowing myself to be muddied with it, is to empower me to carry weights that prevent me from really enjoying life in a natural and, above all, healthy way. In the end, everyone has the burdens they want; no one forces us to do so; we can free ourselves from these weights as we understand that understanding based on knowledge will free the burdens. There is no other help than freedom, which frees us from these burdens. Recognizing and knowing how to forgive everyone and especially ourselves will not lead to a higher level of consciousness, where seeing our reflection will not show that person furious with life, angry with himself or with the world, dissatisfied with everything he has failed to achieve, letting out that fun, kind, happy person who sees in others the good that they can bring to your life, being a reflection of attraction generated by their own energy, rising beyond the human nature that sees with the eyes of the flesh, eyes that only see the moment and live in the past or in the future, lamenting for all that they have suffered or for the dreams that they believe that at some point will rescue them from the state of eternal bitterness in which they are.

People who are usually not honest, faithful, loyal, truthful, respectful, kind, empathetic, or better from a perception of universal values will never be able to understand why they repeat something so many times at the exact moment in their lives. Without being willing to change for change to really happen, they lie to themselves, pretending that they will make a change. Do they want things to change?

Changes cannot be achieved by performing the same actions; it is impossible to overcome the natural person that lives in us without modifying the beliefs that limit us to it. Nothing is a coincidence; it is cause and effect that claim their moment.

Financial, economic, emotional, sentimental, personal, and ideological freedom will only be given to the extent that we undertake real actions that help to invest in us and that will give us the appropriate returns; the returns will come to the extent that we work on ourselves as individuals of great value with our own identity, which is perfectly imperfect so that we do not need to change anything but know that we can continuously improve as we move forward and learn from everything that happens to us. The tests are evaluations that help us face an event in the best way; to solve the problem, we will be able to pass it faster and in the best way. It is not others that make us captive; our minds limit our freedom within themselves. This only lies there, in the mind of each individual, in a personal way, leading to failure or success, making the honey or the gall of their actions prevail in effect as a consequence—consequences of their actions, of their thoughts.

A close person earned very little money a week; I saw her exhausted in her labors, which gave me sadness, and I made her see that there are ways to overcome everything if you have the disposition. She was a young adult at the time, and when I asked her how she would manage to earn more, she did not know what to say. After a few days, she replied, "I know how to earn more." Intriguingly, I kept listening to her say, "I must work another shift!" Unconsciously, I answered, "And yes, do you want to earn triple?"

Carrying the little bags of poop, those weights that, without realizing it, are full of so many things, it is not only the gossip that makes us waste our time; there are countless acts that unwittingly stick in our minds, inner voices, echoes of events that should not concern us. Nowadays, we take this to exaggerated limits of unconsciousness; it is so much what social media, social networks, and the current way of communication (disinformation, in my own words, because we no longer know how to distinguish reality from deceptive appearances) do to alter the way of real appreciation of time, of the human quality of coexistence, and, what is worse, of the true quality of life. Yes, it is true that this helps us to have access to knowledge in a faster way, but it is also true that it brings us closer to a way of interacting that limits us to learning what others think they know and exposing it as true, as fashion, without this leading to a precise, truthful knowledge of the information.

Streams of communication with a lot of disinformation being created as fast as they disappear to entertain without being carefully regulated by those who emit the content, without regulation, are making it fill little bags of poop, heavyweights that have no sense in the lives of all of us, so now I would like us to work three shifts without resting so that this waste of time in absurd images that are leading to an implosion, an explosion inside our being without sense and without benefit, far from growing, we are going backward by leaps and bounds in absurd mentalities, deserted of understanding, taking away the power of learning and giving it to devices that control us at will In other words, should we work two shifts to earn more, or, if we want to earn more, three shifts? Where would the balance be in our lives? That is why the preparation, the healthy development of our emotional intelligence, will help us so that the other bits of intelligence collaborate for the perfect existential growth and development.

Now, people spend hours and hours immersed in meaningless content that doesn't give them a moment of satisfaction but instead makes the algorithms work against them by giving them more and more of everything that makes them interested, curious, or sad. This shows the world who we really are. There it says what kind of content we usually watch, what we like, or catches us to provide us with more of this without allowing brief moments when we want to change the channel, as it used to be done on radio or television. "Wasting time" is a form of weight; it is so much that its heavyweights are destroying those who carry them, creating other priorities, making the poop fill our bags of everything that often does not serve, or rather, most of the time it is "garbage" that cannot even be used for recycling, being aware of others so that they feel they matter, entertaining ourselves with the risks that this implies, exposes us to the fact that at certain times the popular voice cybernetically lynches someone from time to time to claim, as in the Roman circus, the blood of someone so as not to lose the attention of the captive audience that must be held captive,

Without control of those most vulnerable, who are our priorities, as are all the daily activities that we lose for this reason, at those times in which the gossip was limited to taking out the chairs in front of the houses and watching the neighbors pass by, the criticism was limited to a moment of brief recreation and without so much damage. There we returned to daily life at nightfall, invited to rest in order to be ready the next day to carry out all the tasks that implied the individual and responsible lives of each person without pretexts to prevent their being carried out.

We are the result of a lack of education, beliefs, and values that give us access to all these placebos full of information of little value that fill existential and emotional voids that we seek to fill in some way. We have access to create more reprehensible acts shielded on a screen. When I was involved in the gossip about the person who cheated on his partner, well, the story went on. At first, I thought it was fine as long as I knew the truth of this fact and that I had not been the person who said anything about it.

It was none of my interest, none of my business. In fact, I believe that if someone cheats on you, she is not cheating on you; she is cheating on herself. She is not an honest person, let alone a loyal one. She's the one who is letting you down, not you, so I don't think it's due to love; it's more about ego, why me, where did I go wrong, what did I do wrong, and things like that that don't hurt any more than the fait accompli of action by "another" person. We can't control that! In this regard, what we can control are our actions and decisions. Nothing else. So, why suffer for something that is not in our hands because of fear, lack of preparation, loneliness, jealousy, or the feeling that it belongs to us? Any justification is not valid since we are only responsible for what concerns us individually.

So why gossip? Because it abuses our vulnerability, our bad actions, and the shame of facing the consequences. If this person saw it easy, he would relate to another person forgetting his principles, letting himself be carried away by the adrenaline of the moment without thinking about the consequences of his actions, then he would look for a scapegoat to blame for his problems, disguising the reality with the smoke of confusion, hoping to get away with it.

Falling into that saying that a lie told a thousand times... will never become the truth," let's not play that game. In the end, I felt exposed to a reprehensible deed, allowing him to tell me and somehow making me complicit in his actions, carrying the burden by thinking about what end this would have. Then, when it came to light, I was the one who was most damaged by saying that it was an invention of mine. Perfect? To learn the lesson is to understand that we belong to the group and, therefore, we play by the members' own rules, the ones where the majority always wins. Whether you are right or wrong, the joke is to punish someone for the mistakes of others; after all, if someone else is in the same position, they will always look for the weakest to punish someone else's mistake. Why? Because that's the way they get rid of the weakest. Saying that weakness is to be a good person means only that by trying to belong, many times we err in the circle of friends, companions, and friends of dubious values, principles, morals, habits, preparation, and beliefs, and we receive in the right measure what we deserve. Not less, not more; what is fair, whether we like it or not, also has consequences. Even not having a decision is to have a decision. I decide not to be decided at that moment, when the opening is given for the rapacious wolves, the villains, to dominate the game.

Do not do good things that seem bad, and much less bad things that seem good; both are double talk. How do we get out of it simply by doing it, by changing everything that has not worked in the right way? In the end, I faced the situation, and in a moment of great pain, I confronted this person and said, "Ok, I am a gossip, and you?" I am not happy since neither gossip nor deceit are things that cause pain. Therefore, I have tried to stay away from these; if a conversation starts that does not take me anywhere and that lacks value and is of no use to me, then I do not need it, and even less if it starts with "I'll tell you a secret" or "do not tell anyone," it already carries implicit moral damage to someone, and who guarantees me that the game is also played in my direction?

Allow abundance to come into our lives; look for what fills us, makes us happy, and brings well-being to our lives; let's stop carrying that which, by imposition, does not let us move forward. Let's prepare the right way towards the fixed point and look for what we want as a reward—that which is special for us and fills us with peace. It does not matter if others do not understand that the reward differs from what they believe should be obtained. This should be our reward, and we should be fulfilled by it.

In the end, everyone wants to carry what they want because there comes a time when there are so many questions, we ask ourselves and we must answer them, which is both terrifying and comforting at the same time. Since it is the only way of life we know, we are afraid to change because we have played by so many social, family, and cultural rules that limit our understanding. We forget that we are those beings who once had dreams; we thought big; we imagined running around the world being ourselves, without rushing, traveling, creating, and doing what inspired us to achieve our dreams.

Where did all that go when we lost our ideas and started to have bags full of things that limited us? You can't! You shouldn't! That is not for you; you are not that smart; the rules are like that; they impose on you the vision of others, their fears, or, in extreme cases, their frustrated dreams. We become that place where everyone can leave their debris without responding properly, allowing certain programs within us to be triggered. Where do we go if we act badly? We go to hell. If you are not good in their way, then you go against what is marked, where freedom is being conditioned to these limits.

To free ourselves is to go beyond the reality we know, to seek to transcend to something better, to surpass ourselves, and to leave behind those vicious thoughts that fill our minds with garbage, with things that we do not need and that have no value in our lives. Modifying habits means deciding to be better by practicing new ways of being and living in the present moment, not before or after, where anchors prevent us from growing. With this, our self-esteem will begin to grow; we will develop more security, faith, and good spirits that will introduce us to the right path.

We are who we want to be, but what if we are not? We are that reflection, which traps us into creating our best or worst version of ourselves. It is time to reflect on the best version of us, to stop listening to the garbage of others, to put our senses to work, to treasure only that which elevates us, that makes us grateful for every moment that allows us the call to the right action, and to fill ourselves with faith and security.

The garbage is not for us; let us let go of everything that has hurt us, learn to overcome it, and make this energy work in our favor and not against us. Who can say that he is the only person who has suffered? No one, absolutely no one, can have the exclusivity of it. It comes attached to human nature, which, far from being bad, is something that teaches us to create a strength that can save us from ourselves. To overcome the process, one must create a stronger, better, and more authentic person.

Damage is a moment of detriment we go through only for a moment; it depends only on oneself to take that opportunity to decide how we will take it. We are more than this moment, one that can pass and cease to have importance, or we can anchor it in our minds to play that recurring role that makes us suffer, or we can simply see it as something that does not define us and that we can let it go in a simple, uncomplicated way.

Let it go.

Live in the present moment.

Change our mental files.

Find the right way to support ourselves.

Create new ways and changes that lead us to our goals.

Believe and create what we want.

Learn, relearn, and unlearn everything to function better.

Avoid everyone and everything that does not contribute.

to be confident, active, and fearless.

to generate constant knowledge that reaffirms, avoids, modifies, and updates our beliefs.

To have faith, the beliefs that define us.

to let go in the right way, to break attachments.

Avoid everything that is harmful, damaging, aggressive, controlling, or without justification.

To see reality, to observe with our eyes and our senses wide open, we must be alert to any situation we accept or reject in the short, medium, or long term.

to stop victimizing ourselves and to be heroes in our stories.

Put the value of the here and now, leave the past behind, and bring it to the present only to overcome us and bring happiness, and the future will be only to set a fixed point for our achievements, without allowing depression, pain, and anxiety to make us prey.

Learning to speak positively, creating moments that position us with security, security, control, and self-esteem, and filling us with power and value, we are no longer that inner child who fears, suffers, and is insecure about everyone and everything. Becoming great with high self-esteem allows us to move forward with confident steps on the path of life that we have decided to follow.

I am the most important being; I am a beautiful person, wonderful, creative, and creator of everything that generates light, life, and positive energy that produces that acceptance of who I really am; I am perfectly created, complete, I lack nothing, and I can always be better; imperfections do not exist; they are only ways that lead me to be better; they elevate me with the knowledge that helps me to improve. We are the most valuable person in this life.

To be open to help is to accept all the elements and tools that help us move forward and create the progress that allows us to express what is inside us.

Then we learn to understand that the weights that slow our steps are heavyweights that we should not carry. They weigh because the weight is not right for us; it causes bitterness that physically invades our bodies.

Over time, heavy things that limit what we can do creep into our minds in such a way that their weight locks us up.

We are not anyone's puppets; we can move forward on our own without the need for help that forces us to walk paths that we do not want or that do not correspond to us. Let us not allow the direct management of others where the imposition overwhelms us in its path, being aware of the damage while still justifying the actions for reasons that we ourselves do not understand. Nor let it indirectly affect us, letting go of that which is not ours to carry. Heavyweights that drown our own essence, ending not only with our humanity but also with the spiritual creation that seduces us under its control with what is good or bad, reaching the extremes that induce us to produce numbing sensations. Carrying those little bags of poop that begin to invade us in such a way that we can perish with them

The reality is as simple as the habit itself: it is so easy to create habits since we are children that as we grow up, we program ourselves systematically and without control, closing our eyes to reality to not feel pain, and accepting to be clones of others who, with their good desires, limit our vision by altering the environments and introducing programs that are detonated in such a way that they affect the actions we perform.

Not everything is really good or really bad; the bad thing is how we allow extremes to dominate our actions, falling into passivity or euphoria without reaching the middle ground that gives us the peace we need to be able to reason, see the context, and decide whether we want to act or remain oblivious to it. Decisions take on this role so that, even if we do nothing, we are already doing something. Producing consequences of these actions or non-actions. We go from being actors to spectators without consciously understanding what we want...

We want to be happy, achieve our goals, and go out and walk those paths that call us.

What prevents us, we are wonderful people, limited to external circumstances that have marked our interior with insecurity, with that desire to belong, we have forgotten that we belong to ourselves, that is the only clear and real thing that exists, that we avoid to not suffer, staying there for so long in this vicious circle that prevents us from listening to the call to action and motivating us in such a way that takes us out of these beliefs that prevent us from being.

Let's talk about God as our eternal father or about creation, the universe, and creative energy. This always leads us to creation, to going beyond, to growing, and to never staying the same and dying in a life without meaning or purpose. We have been created for this beautiful opportunity that we have called life; therefore, there must be gratitude in it, no matter the means that have intervened for it. Those like us have faced circumstances that, through the ignorance of others, have caused us pain. Yesterday is not today; it is not now, and this can only hurt us as we remember it and bring it into the now that we are living. We are not a memory; we are not a past event. Did we make a mistake? The only way to change it and obtain forgiveness is by recognizing and understanding where that action comes from and correcting it. It has not been our mistake to accept beings equally or more hurt than us, much less to control their actions; what is our mistake is to repeat these patterns without saying: Enough! No more...

To stop is to rebel against the actions of others; it is to save ourselves from these behaviors that, by emotional necessity, lead us to painful situations that trap us in endless spirals of damage, where we can be the victims or the perpetrators. Everything in excess tires hurts controls.

Imagine something as simple as eating; this noble act helps us to grow and maintain a healthy development of our physiological functions, which transcend this, causing mental, physical, and emotional health, which allows us to perform activities as imperceptible as breathing, irrigating through our beautiful blood all our organs, bringing oxygen to every part of our being, and thus giving life to the physical form of our being, making our house, the vehicle that leads us along the path of life, take our being shaped by our spirituality to consciously take their actions to what we should call good and beautiful for us. The universe governs this with its laws and universal values that never change. What is good will always be good, and what is bad will be too. In our excess and ignorance, we fall into errors; these often lead to control, fanaticism, and destruction.

How to avoid them, in a simple way; avoiding the extremes: if I eat in excess, my body will react to it; if I do not eat well, I will cause problems in my whole organism; and if I do not eat, I will cause it not to work, so there will be damage in my being. This vehicle called the body that drives me through life must be properly nourished and cared for in order to achieve my goals.

If we tend to eat a lot, we will not only be overweight but also carry a heavier weight, which not only affects our self-esteem but also sees us constantly in that complaint, programming our words to I am fat, "the clothes do not fit me, and "I must exercise, and that is not the solution. The solution lies in what we eat; there will be no exercise that works if we do not first control how we eat; only then will we become aware, and our minds will reprogram our way of interacting with food. Believe it or not? It can also be part of our need for affection, where sweetness leads us to feel somehow that pleasure that supplants voids that we want to fill.

On the other hand, a lack of nourishment is the opposite and equally destructive way that also takes us to the limits, where we access obscure thoughts that alter the perception of reality. Both are states that scream something that is not right within us. They are escapes; they are outlets we use as distractors from emotions, feelings, or needs, forgetting that we are not alone. We have ourselves; that should be enough. It is enough. To learn to understand loneliness, we must understand that we can talk to ourselves; to learn to live with others in a good way, we must first learn to have a healthy coexistence with ourselves. If we achieve this, we will avoid these extremes that make us hurt others or allow them to hurt us.

Food is just one example of the extremes we all tend to go to. These are radical; they forget respect for everyone, for everything... My space ends when the space of others begins, so my space must be respected, and I must respect the space of others without imposing my beliefs. What I believe only concerns me, so if I can expose, express, and accept that there will be those who agree with my ideals, beliefs, views, ethnicity, preferences, culture, etc., there are so many factors involved in diversity where respect and empathy make us feel the universal values without wanting to adapt them to a fashion or social or cultural trend. These are the ones that make it simpler for us to resist going to extremes and radicalizing our behaviors, which the vox populi may occasionally encourage by carrying us along like paper boats in the currents of water without our consent.

Understanding that we have all been children, parents, siblings, grandparents, teachers, and tutors should give us the responsibility to help others without instilling beliefs that stop them from learning in a healthy way. This should make us think about our actions instead of putting heavyweights on them that can kill them. Just as many times, we have been the pack mules of those who have mercilessly limited us to it.

If food is not a good example, we could say that even the best people have had their black moments," where, because they wanted everything to be perfect, they fell into intolerance, leading them to perform not very good acts that contradicted their purposes or principles. There is a saying that goes: "The end justifies the means," and it is not true; what it does is that we play the same game in such a way that it becomes a norm, a "normal" way of doing things, something that becomes public domain and is adopted in a cultural way, not because it is good; simply by repetition it stops being evaluated, modified, creating a use that gives a general custom to a fact that allows the community to make it its law. What is good for some will not be good for others, and that is why it is good to base ourselves on the universal laws and their principles, which can be found in the natural conscience of each of us. When we are small, we are so close to our spirituality that we forgive very quickly, forget without rancor, and believe again.

We see life without those weights, which in many ways we want to avoid; they are imposed on us, and after five minutes, we leave them behind; we do not want to carry them, and something inside tells us that it is not right. We're so sensitive to other people's pain that it makes us want to comfort them and make them smile in the face of trouble. However, this same sensitivity makes us vulnerable to the worst kinds of damage when we're not paying attention. Even so, we're able to recover from it by the time we're adults, and we keep it in our minds, repeating the damage in such a way that we fall into excesses, grossness, malnutrition, and other extremes that hurt us. To leave the past behind is to see the opportunity, run to meet it, and pay the price; in the end, the reward will be worth it; it will always be better than captivity.

We should not last forty years in the desert for the traditions to be forgotten, for the pain to pass, and for a better generation to rise again. This is our time. Let's shine our light so brightly that it touches other people and makes them want to change for the better. We can do this by being the kind of people who make mistakes but learn from them and who, in tests, are put through the strongest pressures that make the most beautiful diamonds. Never will the impurities be lost if we do not evidence them in such a way that they embarrass us; only by overcoming this moment will we know how to magnify the person that we really are. In this act, there will not only be greatness, but also the power that leads to places of peace, with the happiness that avoids small moments of bitterness by fading them immediately with positive thoughts, changing our gaze to another place, and trying to destroy the way our mind activates that memory by taking its energy and using it in our favor. Winning is not about losses. Winning is about being better. Producing will be about reducing what is useless, discarding it, and leaving that space for something that generates.

Whether we like it or not, it will take its toll. How can we learn something new if we have both hands occupied, one in the past and the other in the future? None of these moments are in the now, so letting go is to open our hands to this instant and take it in such a way that it makes us feel alive, that we can be grateful for the moment, and escape from everything that has been hindering our growth. Sometimes they will be things that have a special value or people that we think we love, so letting go is to think well about the value and the consequences without trying to justify selfish, blind justifications that are partial. To see reality naturally without false performances and learn to decide, pay the price, and receive the reward.

To be the person we want to be, we must know how to choose the food we should put in our mouths. In the end, we will be what we eat, what we see, what we think, and what we expose ourselves to. This will reflect the life we have and expose who we are, no matter how much we want to pretend!

There will always be those moments that reveal who we really are. It is in these moments that, if they are not correct acts, we must turn on the alerts to change and get out of there; it is no coincidence that the value of copper valued by experts will never be compared to gold.

The challenge is for us to either live in darkness or bring to light our beauty. This is to stop carrying heavy weights and carry loads that lighten our walk through life, letting go of the past and the future to have empty hands, open to everything beautiful, good, and excellent that life has for us, stopping eating what does not nourish us, no matter how tasty it may have seemed to us so far, to stop feeling that it is a priority, not to live to eat, on the contrary, it is to know how to eat to live in the right way, not to see an enemy, and to know that not eating is also a lack of nourishment in our lives, so that balance will give us the strength to do everything in the right way.

There is no end; simply by transcending, ascending, and advancing, we achieve the full development that leads us to exaltation, thus creating not only contact with other people who, like us, are also seeking to lighten their burdens but also impact their lives in the right way.

Contact + impact = transcend

To go beyond achieving is to bring out the happiness that remains within us as that endless force that will give us satisfaction and the peace that makes everything calm.

The burdens are heavy not because of their size or weight; they are heavy because of the words that give them that power. That weight comes from the limitations they create in our minds, which make us believe that we cannot carry them, without realizing that we are carrying the problem rather than the burden and believing that the solution is to find a way to carry it.

CONCLUSION

Loving is a feeling that puts us in the highest degree of perception; beyond an appearance, this is a reality that makes us see a part of ourselves that tells us who we are; the rest has that dark side that we do not usually resort to for fear of feeling bad. However, it is stalking us so that it eats away at our minds, so we tend to repress it to be socially accepted, believing that we are well and judging others exceptionally harshly. We hate that part of ourselves that we see reflected in others. The ones we ignore don't bother us because they're not part of us. What checks you shock you.

To live with our eyes closed is to live in an unreal world, allowing that dark side that we carry within us to justify us, allowing our unconscious to take over in such a way that, by escaping public shame, we explain it, making ourselves extremely hard to deal with when it comes to judging, offending others, feeling that they deserve it, abusing our power, becoming vulnerable, and allowing abuse, both of which are damages that are done to justify some unworked trauma, victimize oneself, or justify oneself before what has no justification: losing the reality and objectivity of the dark part that we all carry and that we only control is to belong and play the rules that are imposed on us. Looking for the opportunity to experience those biases of the morally correct that lead us to experience in a wrong way what worries us, attracts us, or limits us Without being able to be ourselves, we cannot be what we want without affecting others or causing them harm. We remember the respect and space that begin where ours ends.

We are not saviors of the world; we can find a way to help without falling into impositions that attack the individuality of others, so looking inside ourselves and knowing who we really are and what we want to change or control cannot make us free. We need rules and rules that allow us to overcome those barriers of confusion that limit our progress. Inside us, we know that it is the best; what we do not want to hear is what usually bothers us, what makes us bitter. Allow us to be special and unique. Therefore, we must maintain control of what makes us wild by controlling that being that wants the reins to always leave it limited to not giving the extra, to the mediocrity of existence of half beliefs. He half believes that he can, half believes that he achieves it, and half does it without ever opening himself to new opportunities with frustrated dreams and goals never achieved.

If we didn't feel like we had to repeat experiences, we wouldn't be married so many times to the same person with different names. Letting someone special come into our lives opens us up to real life and lets us use the best of our genes to be and to pass on.

Each one is as he is because of what he has lived, because of the time or the circumstances, and inside he carries his truth; this will not change until he decides to change it, from the inside, from the conscious, silencing those voices that for years have finished us off. Victimize at will.

We are more than a simple process of actions; we are energy, we are the creation, and our duty goes beyond a small existential moment.

I tend to think that religions have a wonderful power in people as long as they are not radical; they can manage to concentrate many energies at the same time that come together in the same harmony, with a spirit of goodness, wanting to do and receive all the good that can be done, achieving with this forgiveness the release of those weights that we are subject to carry. And the truth will make us free, and by being free, we will recognize the power of our creation.

We are wonderful, perfect beings who want to go beyond ourselves by getting better. We are whole and can learn new things, improving our skills and turning our weaknesses into strengths.

Meditate, learn, change, achieve, and do it; there is no tomorrow, only today now; forgive, live, let live, and gather in your life experience a wonderful selection of experiences, looking for the best ways to achieve it, with the experts, with the better, being excellence, the sight of my triumph, and that the desire of the goal only matters to you, that it makes you happy, fills you with fullness and peace to continue, to feel, and most importantly, to project without fear, which you are.

I am grateful that everything is given the way it should be, without so much that makes me feel superior or with so little that makes me feel unhappy. Leaving my ego aside and filling my feelings with deep love makes me thank and recognize how beautiful life can be if we are with the right people, in perfect harmony, living in the present, giving as many hugs and kisses as recognition and help to what is at this moment keeping us company. Let ourselves be carried away by the spiritual energy that allows us to see beyond the established norms, break paradigms, and achieve everything we want. To this, I express my deep gratitude. Thank you for not allowing me to wander my way to perdition, pulling me, motivating me, and demanding in the right way that I see the best of myself and that this will project it, attracting this comforting peace that does not let me stay too long in a state that hurts me or hurts those I love. If this happens, it will be part of his learning, freeing me from that concern of having done something wrong.

Seeing the light at the end of the tunnel encourages me to keep going, move forward, vibrate in the right way, and realize that my energy is always moving toward eternal progress.

Excellence is the calling that all human beings have. Free ourselves from toxic energies that prevent us from feeling freedom.

My mother used to get up in the morning thanking and blessing every corner of the house and her children, and she expressed her deep concern that wrong actions or energies could cause something serious. Poverty, problems, bad energy, loss, or heartbreak often lie in wait for us to look for a moment of weakness and take advantage of it, quickly taking over the situation.

Arguments and lawsuits are evils that eat away at the vision, seeking to win a war with blood, pain, and anguish and believing themselves to be winners.

The environment is not his. It is what we are wearing in, where we fill our houses, work environments, and environments with those energies that they absorb and emit, subsequently contaminating our environments—acting on us and those who dwell or inhabit there. So, with the world. We generate what we ask of the universe.

For the most part, they are signs that we can perceive, both happiness and abundance and their counterparts, chaos and bitterness.

My mother expressed that the plants dry up, the glass breaks, the environment remains dark or has a thick air that identifies negative energies, there are cracks in the doors, the pipes are spoiled, and they capture the discomfort of the people. So she was looking for a way that would always counteract this and make us sensitive to it. Cleaning is the beginning of everything, not only of the area, the house, and the environment but also of the mind; letting evil thoughts out is not bad. It isn't good to keep them inside, weighing you down.

She used to say that good deeds are like sharp knives or scissors that are supposed to counteract this energy, making it perish.

She never stopped being active in her life, and abundance used to be something she always attracted. Mirrors, plants, and pets usually catch the bad that one generates or others want to invade our lives in our houses and environments, so that the attraction is generated in a forced way towards the good, that which gives light, clarity, cleanliness, without accumulating pain or useless things. He threw away everything he received from us. Having something material is something of value to the one who gives it to you. Still, it has no more weight than the one who gives it to you.

The certainty of this is that abundance comes when there is a place for it; we must let go of what we have to grab what comes to us. If a glass is empty, it can be filled, but if it is full of something, we must put plenty of liquid in it so that it ends up removing all the above and giving space to the new liquid, which must be better.

So now that I understand this, I must say that if my feelings are fighting to be better, I must make the good feelings stronger until the intensity I want is modified. With all our abilities, we will see, hear, and feel the reality of the surroundings more intensely and better. We will stop living on automatic and getting hooked on those explosions that make us exaggerate how we act. Keeping control, meditating, and analyzing are ways to start gaining self-knowledge, self-control, and self-perception, so we will be the ones to understand our emotional intelligence, neurolinguistic programming, beliefs, capacities, skills, and talents that will make our limitations diminish in the face of greatness. Of our being, we understand that we are energy, light, that has harmony with the beautiful, the good, and the noble that brings within this happiness that can flood our life.

GRATITUDE

Thanks to my parents' love for allowing me to never limit my abilities and their rudeness for making me understand the language of intelligence that prevails in me and the way to adapt to all environments, that understanding forms a film that goes with me. Reality and not that of others. To my brothers for their incredible intelligence and displays of affection.

Thanks to my beloved daughters and my darling son, who put me in constant motion without letting me beat or stop at anything and who have lived by my side through all the events that tested the actual person I am and the way to overcome myself, And grow to my grandchildren: Blanca, Karla, Carlos, Nany, Pepe, Neny, Elias, Yayi, Tocha, Mimina, and Carlo. That is the union they have made, where the balance is always level, without excesses, neither towards the bad nor the good, where the ego makes us prey to nothing, where someone always seeks to mediate and remain in harmony.

Thanks to the love that touches my life in a personal way, it has given me the opportunity at this moment to finish and learn things that I put on hold due to the hectic way I had to live. To my husband, who helps me to be better and to understand more, and here today, on this occasion, he has shown me that accompaniment goes beyond signs of love; it brings respect to the uniqueness of us, to the support between us, and to the inspiration that has left me with the motivation.

To achieve what I like beyond the disposition with total commitment, Steve Smith.

Thanks to my great teacher, who knew who I was and motivated me to be who I am without being ashamed of it, making me feel that in my madness there was greatness in wanting to free myself from the rules that regulate individual identity, we were friends, family, and excellent companions. Of work, those that allowed us to stimulate progress beyond everything. He knew my way of learning and how to direct it to his benefit and, therefore, mine. I miss you; as much as these happen, I can never imagine life without you. I usually feel you, and I perceive your smell. I miss that smile that used to disappear in worry, but I never allowed this to affect the family union. Ernesto.

For everything, I usually give thanks since everyone in my life has had a reason that has taught me something; what I can regret is not having had the necessary understanding to make them feel my gratitude and recognize who they are for me and the influence this leaves on me.

Continually cut the environment that becomes negative, cross those limits that do not allow me to see, hear, or perceive correctly, and be in that place every moment in the present time, with open eyes, controlling the wild way that pulls me to the primitive, to the primary emotions that should not prevail, basing the pure, clean, strong feelings as a fixed part of my programming and letting them become natural.

Thank you, God, for the moment of life that I receive from you to the universe full of knowledge that I can access, to that energy that creates, and to the fact that with faith I remain on the good paths that lead me to be good, better, and excellent, managing to find my continuous way to eternal improvement.

MY STORY

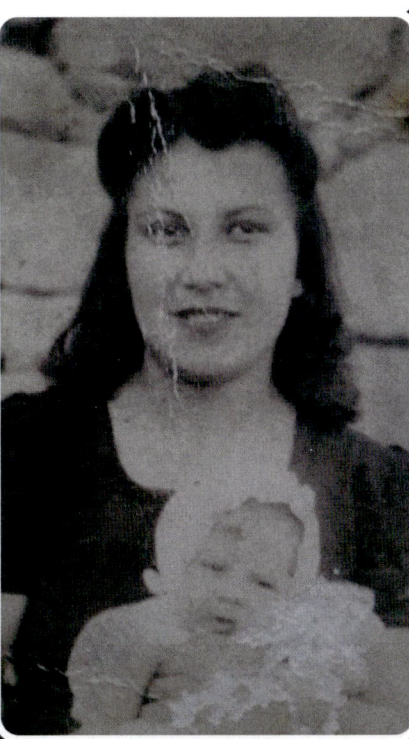

MY STORY

MY STORY

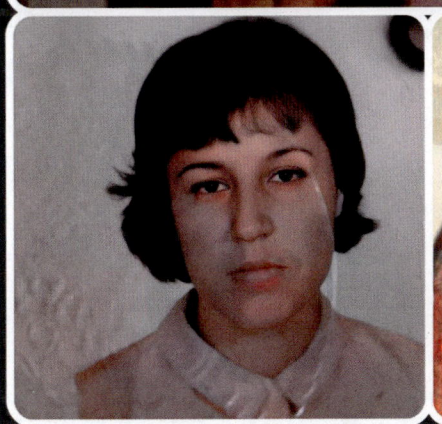

MY STORY

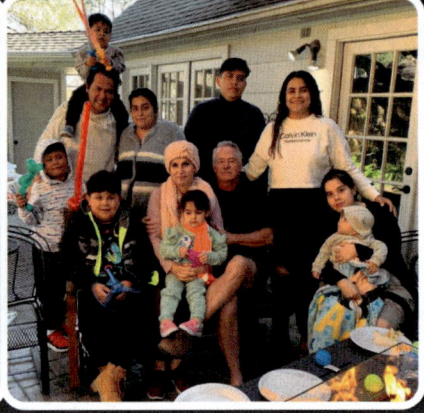

MY STORY

MY STORY

MY STORY

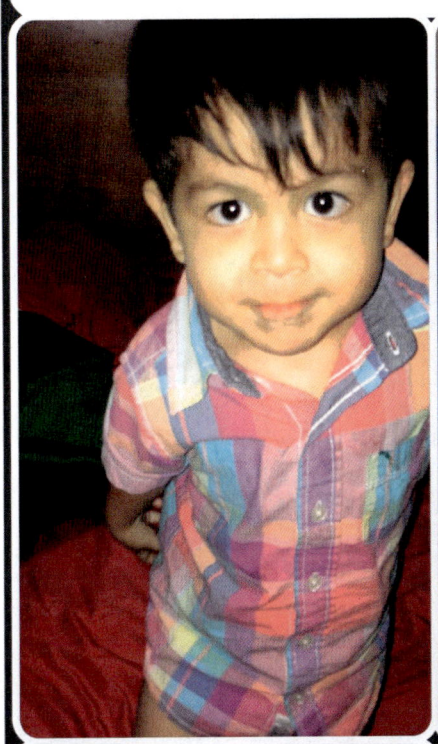

MY STORY

MY STORY

MY STORY

BIBLIOGRAPHY / REFERENCES

1. Paradoxes: fact or expression apparently contrary to logic; another entry containing the form.

paradox, paradox | Definition | Spanish language dictionary | RAE - ASALE

2. Succumb:

3. There is an anonymous story of the Cherokee Indians that goes like this: "An old man of the tribe tells his granddaughter about a fight that occurs inside him. He tells her that it is a fight between two wolves. One is evil, rage, envy, sadness, resentment, greed, arrogance, self-pity, guilt, resentment, inferiority, lies, false pride, heartbreak, superiority, and ego. The other is goodness, joy, peace, love, hope, serenity, humility, kindness, benevolence, empathy, generosity, truth, compassion, and faith. The granddaughter thinks for a few minutes and asks the grandfather:

"Which of the two wins?"

The old sage simply answers:

"The one I feed."

The wolves that inhabit us – www.fragacarlos.com

4. Gregarious: living in a group or herd.

gregarious, gregarious | Definition | Spanish language dictionary | RAE - ASALE

5. Chaos: confusion or disorder.

chaos | Definition | Spanish language dictionary | RAE - ASALE

6. Bible, Matthew 19:14

And, Jesus said: "Let the little children come to me and do not prevent them from doing so, for of such belongs the kingdom of heaven."

King James Version Matthew 19:14 - Search

7. The law of action and reaction or Isaac Newton's third law, States that forces always appear because of the interaction between two bodies. In other words, the action of a force on a body cannot be manifested without another body causing it. Furthermore, in such an interaction, the forces always appear in pairs.

Action and reaction or Newton's third law (leerciencia.net)

8. The law of cause and effect is one of the most powerful laws in the universe, it is the idea that every action has a reaction or consequence. It's a basic principle of physics: for every action, there is an equal and opposite reaction. This law is what governs our lives, it also applies to our thoughts and actions.

The Law Of Cause And Effect: How It Affects Your Life – Expand Your Mind

9. "The science of love", by the psychiatrist A. García-Castrillón.

The Science of Love – Crowdcast

10. The madman (publicdomain.es)

GIBRÁN KHALIL GIBRÁN

THE MADMAN (1918)

You ask me how I went crazy. This is how it happened: One day, long before the gods were born, I woke up from a deep sleep and discovered that all my masks had been stolen - yes; the seven masks that I myself had made, and that I wore in seven different lives-; I ran without a mask through the crowded streets, shouting: -Thieves! Burglars! Damned thieves! Men and women laughed at me, and seeing me, several people, full of fear, ran to take refuge in their houses. And when I arrived at the market square, a young man, standing on the roof of his house, pointing at me, shouted: -Look! He is crazy! I raised my head to see who was screaming, and for the first time the sun kissed my naked face, and my soul was inflamed with love for the sun, and I no longer wanted to have masks. And as if caught in a trance, I shouted: -Blessed! Blessed are the thieves who stole my masks! So it was that I became crazy. And in my madness I have found freedom and security; the freedom of solitude and the security of not being understood, because those who understand us enslave a part of our being. But don't let me take too much pride in my safety; not even the jailed thief is safe from another thief.

11. Crowded: adjective that expresses a high presence of something or someone.

Definition of Attestation » Concept in Definition ABC (definicionabc.com)

12. Crazy: person who has lost reason, judgment; reckless, reckless.

crazy, crazy | Definition | Spanish language dictionary | RAE - ASALE

13. Gregarious: living in herds or groups, united.

gregarious, gregarious | Definition | Spanish language dictionary | RAE - ASALE

14. Newton's third law (or principle of action and reaction) that says: if a body exerts a force on another body, the first body receives a force applied by the

second body of the same value, but in the opposite direction.

▷ Newton's third law (principle of action and reaction) (engineering.com)

15. Haters

Social media haters: who are they? - RG Municipality Blog (riogrande.gob.ar)

However, this revolution has also brought with it negative consequences, such as Internet addiction, cyberbullying, or the exercise of haters, among others. This term, imported from English, refers to someone who hates or abhors. And it is used in social networks to name users who systematically attack others on the web.

Haters despise, defame or destructively criticize a person, entity, or work. They are those individuals who, to express themselves on any subject, use mockery, irony, and black humor.

16. Postponed: leave something behind.

postpone | Definition | Spanish language dictionary | RAE - ASALE

17. "Monsters are real, ghosts too: they live inside us and sometimes they win." Stephen King

monsters and demons exist live inside us - Search (bing.com)

18. Phrases of Pedro Paramo:

—Me here, by the door looking at the sunrise and watching when you left, following the path of heaven; where the sky began to open up in lights, moving you away, more and more faded among the shadows of the earth.

19. Quotes from The Little Prince:

"It's crazy to hate all the roses because one pricked you." Give up all dreams because one did not come true.

—I lived a lot with elderly people and I have known them very closely, but this has not improved my opinion of them.

20. The Fox and the Little Prince

-Come to play with me! I'm very sad... —said the little prince remembering his rose.

"I can't, I'm not domesticated."

"What is taming?" Seeking friends...

"To have a friend you must tame him." tame me!

-And what is there to do?

—It's something like always being at the right time and place, to create a connection, so I'll come at the same time to wait for you. The time you spent with your rose is what made you love her.

"Goodbye," said the fox, "but first I'm going to tell you my secret: you can't see well except with your heart." The essential is invisible to the eyes.

"What is essential is invisible to the eye," the Little Prince repeated to remind him.

"Men have forgotten this secret, but you must remember it." You are responsible for whom you have tamed forever.

They have forgotten.

21. Phrases about lawyers:

"Lawyers are men we hire to protect us from other lawyers.

"A lawyer with his briefcase can rob more than a hundred men with guns."

—Sometimes I criticize lawyers, but I reconsider my remarks when I need the services of one.

"Lawyers are the only people not punished for ignorance of the law.

30 phrases of lawyers | 10.top phrases

22. 55 famous Jiddu Krishnamurti quotes (on life and love) (estilonext.com)

23. Flattery: Affected praise to gain someone's will.

flattery | Definition | Spanish language dictionary | RAE - ASALE

24. Bags, several meanings but we are going to use two:

1) Stupid, stupid person.

bags | Definition | Spanish language dictionary | RAE - ASALE

2) Kind of bag or sack of cloth or other material, used to carry or store something.

bag | Definition | Spanish language dictionary | RAE – ASALE

ImagiLab

Made in the USA
Columbia, SC
24 March 2023